First World War
and Army of Occupation
War Diary
France, Belgium and Germany

33 DIVISION
19 Infantry Brigade
Queen's (Royal West Surrey Regiment)
1st Battalion
1 February 1918 - 15 May 1919

WO95/2422/1

The Naval & Military Press Ltd
www.nmarchive.com
Published in association with The National Archives

Published by

The Naval & Military Press Ltd

Unit 10 Ridgewood Industrial Park,

Uckfield, East Sussex,

TN22 5QE England

Tel: +44 (0) 1825 749494

www.naval-military-press.com

www.nmarchive.com

This diary has been reprinted in facsimile from the original. Any imperfections are inevitably reproduced and the quality may fall short of modern type and cartographic standards.

© **Crown Copyright**
Images reproduced by permission of The National Archives, London, England, 2015.

Contents

Document type	Place/Title	Date From	Date To
Heading	WO95/2422/1 1Bn. Queens (R. West Suneg) Regt. 1918 Feb-1919 May		
Heading	33rd Division 19th Infy Bde. 1st Bn (Queen's) Roy. West Surrey Regt. Feb 1918-May 1919		
War Diary	Setques	01/02/1918	05/02/1918
War Diary	Longuenesse	06/02/1918	19/02/1918
War Diary	St. Jean Camp.	20/02/1918	21/02/1918
War Diary	Support Line D166/5.35.	21/02/1918	25/02/1918
War Diary	St. Jean Camp.	25/02/1918	28/02/1918
War Diary		12/03/1918	15/03/1918
War Diary	St Jean Camp	16/03/1918	18/03/1918
War Diary	Toronto Camp	19/03/1918	21/03/1918
War Diary	Irksome	21/03/1918	27/03/1918
War Diary	St. Lawrence Camp	27/03/1918	31/03/1918
Heading	19th Brigade. 33rd Division. 1st Battalion The Queen's (Royal West Surrey) Regiment April 1918.		
War Diary		01/04/1918	05/04/1918
War Diary	Y Camp Duisans	06/04/1918	07/04/1918
War Diary	Beaufort	08/04/1918	11/04/1918
War Diary	Meteren	11/04/1918	14/04/1918
War Diary	Noote Boom	15/04/1918	19/04/1918
War Diary	St. Jans Capel	19/04/1918	21/04/1918
War Diary	Campagne Dreve	22/04/1918	30/04/1918
Heading	19th Brigade. 33rd Division. War Diary & Appendices. 1st Battalion The Queen's Royal West Surrey Regiment April 1918.		
Miscellaneous	Awards. Appendix I		
Miscellaneous	Standing Orders For Move	10/12/1918	10/12/1918
Heading	19th Brigade. 33rd Division. Report On Operations Etc. 1st Battalion "The Queen's) R.W. Surrey) Regiment April 1918.		
Miscellaneous Map	Position Of Sheet 27 S.E. 1:20,000 Enlarged t 1:10,000.		
Miscellaneous Map	Position of Sheet 27 SE 1:20,000 Enlarged t 1:10,000.		
Miscellaneous Map	Position of Sheet 27 SE 1:20,000 Enlarged t 1:10,000.		
Miscellaneous Map	Position of Sheet 27 S.E. (Belgium & Part of France) 1:20,000. enlarged to 1:10,000.		
Miscellaneous Map	App II. Showing In Red Positions		
Miscellaneous	Operations South of Meteren 12-14/April/1918.	12/04/1918	12/04/1918
Miscellaneous	Appendix I		
Operation(al) Order(s)	Battalion Order No. 70 by Lt: Col: M.Kemp-Welsh D.S.O., M.C. Comdg. Bn: "The Queen"S" Regiment.	05/04/1918	05/04/1918
Miscellaneous	Battalion Orders by L-Col. M. Kemp-Welch. D.S.O., M.G. Comdg. Bn. The Queen's Regt.	16/04/1918	16/04/1918
Operation(al) Order(s)	Battalion Orders No. 81 by Lt. Col. M.Kemp-Welch, D.S.O., M.C. Comdg. The Queen's	14/04/1918	14/04/1918

Type	Description	Date From	Date To
Operation(al) Order(s)	Battalion Order No. 83 by Lieut Col.M.Kemp Welsh D.S.O., M.C. Comdg 1 Bn. The Queen, Regt.	19/04/1918	19/04/1918
Operation(al) Order(s)	Battalion Order No. 84. By Lieut. Col. M.Kemp Welsh D.S.O., M.C. Comdg. 1 Bn The Queen's Regt.	20/04/1918	20/04/1918
Miscellaneous	Battalion Order No. by Lieut. Col. M.Kemp Welsh D.S.O. M.C. Comdg Bn the Queen's Regiment	29/04/1918	29/04/1918
Miscellaneous	Appendix V	30/04/1918	30/04/1918
Miscellaneous			
War Diary	Racquinghem	01/05/1918	03/05/1918
War Diary	Sheet 27 L. 8.c. 2.5.	04/05/1918	05/05/1918
War Diary	G 21 b.	06/05/1918	08/05/1918
War Diary	G. 30.D.5.8.	08/05/1918	09/05/1918
War Diary	G.30.D.5.8.		
War Diary	N.3.D.4.5.		
War Diary	N.3.D.4.5.	09/05/1918	10/05/1918
War Diary	G 21b & Dirty Bucket Camp A.30.Central	11/05/1918	14/05/1918
War Diary	Dirty Bucket Camp (A.30. Central)	15/05/1918	17/05/1918
War Diary	K 12 b	18/05/1918	23/05/1918
War Diary	G.11.d. 4.2.	24/05/1918	02/06/1918
War Diary	Rainsford Camp K 12 b. 6.4.	03/06/1918	07/06/1918
War Diary	28/H.23.b.	08/06/1918	11/06/1918
War Diary	28/H 15.b. 9.5.	12/06/1918	13/06/1918
War Diary	28/H.18. D.4.2.	13/06/1918	15/06/1918
War Diary	28/H.7.c.7.0.	16/06/1918	20/06/1918
War Diary	H.23.d	21/06/1918	23/06/1918
War Diary	H.23 d. L.14.a.0.2.	23/06/1918	24/06/1918
War Diary	H.23 d.	25/06/1918	25/06/1918
War Diary	H.23 d. L.14.a.0.2.	26/06/1918	27/06/1918
War Diary	H.23.d K3d.	28/06/1918	30/06/1918
War Diary	G 11 d 1.2.	01/07/1918	01/07/1918
War Diary	K 3 d.	01/07/1918	04/07/1918
War Diary	Front Line Bn H.Q. H 24.b.4.8	05/07/1918	08/07/1918
War Diary	Support Battn H.Q H.15.b.9.5.	09/07/1918	09/07/1918
War Diary	Support H.15.b.9.5.	09/07/1918	15/07/1918
War Diary	Divn. Reserve G.11d.	16/07/1918	20/07/1918
War Diary	Front Line & H.Q. H 24.c	21/07/1918	27/07/1918
War Diary	Support H 23 d.	28/07/1918	30/07/1918
War Diary	Erie Farm	30/07/1918	31/07/1918
War Diary	Erie Farm 28/H.11.D.O.1.	01/08/1918	04/08/1918
War Diary	H. 24.b.6.9.	04/08/1918	07/08/1918
War Diary	28/H.24.b.6.9.	08/08/1918	14/08/1918
War Diary	K Nollys Fm 28/H.7.c.	14/08/1918	15/08/1918
War Diary	Husband Camp 28/L.7.D.2.2.	16/08/1918	16/08/1918
War Diary	Husband Camp 27/L.7.D.2.2.	16/08/1918	19/08/1918
War Diary	Mentque	19/08/1918	20/08/1918
War Diary	Sanghen	20/08/1918	26/08/1918
War Diary	Seninghem	27/08/1918	29/08/1918
War Diary	Ivergny (Lens,11. 1/100,000)	29/08/1918	30/08/1918
War Diary	Ivergny	30/08/1918	31/08/1918
War Diary	Ivergny (Lens 11 1/100,000.	01/09/1918	12/09/1918
War Diary	Ivergny	13/09/1918	15/09/1918
War Diary	Front Line	15/09/1918	17/09/1918
War Diary	Manancourt	18/09/1918	19/09/1918
War Diary	Front Line X 19 C 3.2.	20/09/1918	22/09/1918
War Diary	V 17 a	23/09/1918	27/09/1918
War Diary	X.13.c.	28/09/1918	28/09/1918

Type	Description	Start	End
War Diary	W 18 d.	29/09/1918	30/09/1918
War Diary	W 18 d.3.9.	01/10/1918	03/10/1918
War Diary	X 22 b 8.0	04/10/1918	05/10/1918
War Diary	S.14.b.8.2.	06/10/1918	08/10/1918
War Diary	S 16.d. 9.4.	09/10/1918	09/10/1918
War Diary	O.29 b 8.4.	09/10/1918	09/10/1918
War Diary	P 3d 9.6.	10/10/1918	12/10/1918
War Diary	Malincourt. T 5a 80.15.	13/10/1918	14/10/1918
War Diary	Malincourt	15/10/1918	19/10/1918
War Diary	Troisvilles	20/10/1918	22/10/1918
War Diary	N.E. of Le Cateau	22/10/1918	26/10/1918
War Diary	Troisvilles	29/10/1918	04/11/1918
War Diary	Englefontaine	04/11/1918	05/11/1918
War Diary	B 5.a. 6.6.	06/11/1918	06/11/1918
War Diary	Aulnoye Station	06/11/1918	07/11/1918
War Diary	Ecuelin	08/11/1918	08/11/1918
War Diary	Berliamont	08/11/1918	19/11/1918
War Diary	Clary	20/11/1918	11/12/1918
War Diary	Masnieres	11/12/1918	12/12/1918
War Diary	Hermies	12/12/1918	13/12/1918
War Diary	Favreuil	13/12/1918	14/12/1918
War Diary	Albert	14/12/1918	15/12/1918
War Diary	Allonville	15/12/1918	15/12/1918
War Diary	Allonville Breilly	16/12/1918	17/12/1918
War Diary	Camps.	18/12/1918	31/12/1918
Operation(al) Order(s)	Battalion Orders No.255 by Major H.B. Avery M.C. Commanding Bn The Queen's Regt	10/12/1918	10/12/1918
Operation(al) Order(s)	Battalion Orders No. 256 by Major H.B. Avery M.C. Comdg Bn. the Queen's Regt.	11/12/1918	11/12/1918
Operation(al) Order(s)	Battalion Orders No. 257 by Major H.B. Avery M.C. Comdg Bn.The Queen's Regt.	12/12/1918	12/12/1918
Operation(al) Order(s)	Battalion Order No. 258. by Major N.B. Avery M.C. Comdg. Bn. The Queens Regt	13/12/1918	13/12/1918
Operation(al) Order(s)	Battalion Order No 259 by Major N.B. Avery. M.C Comdg. Bn. The Queen's Regt.	14/12/1918	14/12/1918
Operation(al) Order(s)	Battalion Order No. 260 by Major N.B. Avery M.C. Comdg Bn. The Queens Regt	15/12/1918	15/12/1918
Operation(al) Order(s)	Battalion Order No. 261 by Major N.B. Avery M.C. Comdg. Batt The Queens. Regt	16/12/1918	16/12/1918
Heading	1/Queen go to 98th Inf Bde.		
War Diary	Camps	01/01/1919	04/01/1919
War Diary	Havre	05/01/1919	13/01/1919
War Diary	No 17 Camp Harfleur	14/01/1919	25/01/1919
War Diary	Harfleur No 2 Reception Camp	26/01/1919	31/01/1919
Miscellaneous	List Of Officer And Other Ranks Who Were Presented With Medical Ribands by Divisional Commander On 1st January 1919.	01/01/1919	01/01/1919
Operation(al) Order(s)	Battalion Order No. 275 By Lieut Col R Bellamy D.S.O. Comdg. 1st B. The Queens Regt	02/01/1919	02/01/1919
War Diary	Harfleur	01/02/1919	28/02/1919
War Diary	No.2 Reception Camp Harfleur	01/03/1919	15/03/1919
War Diary	Harfleur	16/03/1919	31/03/1919
Operation(al) Order(s)	Battalion Routine Order No. 62. by Lieut-Colonel R. Bellamy D.S.O., Comdg: 1st Battalion "The Queen's Regiment.	13/03/1919	13/03/1919
War Diary	Harfleur	01/04/1919	15/05/1919

WO 95 2422/1

1 Bn. Queens (R. West Surrey) Regt

1918 Feb - 1919 May

33RD DIVISION
19TH INFY BDE

1ST BN (QUEEN'S)
ROY. WEST SURREY REGT.
FEB 1918-MAY 1919

FROM 100 BDE   33 DIV

33RD DIVISION
19TH INFY BDE

WAR DIARY

INTELLIGENCE SUMMARY.

1st Bn. THE QUEEN'S Regt.

FEBRUARY 1918 — Army Form C. 2118.

Page 1

Place	Date	Hour	Summary of Events and Information	Remarks and references to Appendices
SETQUES	1		Training & general routine	W A O
	2		Training & general routine	
	3		Batt. paraded for Church service, took place in the hut in W. S. village	
	4		Training & general routine. Reinforcement of 4 Officers & 119 O.R. joined Batt. from Base Bn. The Queen's. The officers were Lt. H.E.L. Dine, 2 Lt. Stevenson, 2 Lt. R.H.P. Hipps, 2 Lt. H.G. Welch. Lt. Col. W.B.R. Sladen rejoined Batt & resumed command. Orders issued from 100th Inf. Bde for the move of Batt. 5/9th Bn. The Batts. orders for move to LONGUENESSE issued.	2 S1/R-t
	5		Batt. formed up first N.B. village at 10.30 a.m. and proceeded	

WAR DIARY
INTELLIGENCE SUMMARY. 1st Bn. THE QUEEN'S Regt.

Army Form C. 2118. FEBRUARY 1918. PAGE 2

Place	Date	Hour	Summary of Events and Information	Remarks and references to Appendices
LONGUENESSE	6.		Brig. Gen. A.W.F. BAIRD, CMG, DSO, GOC 100th L. Bde delivered farewell address. The Battalion then marched KONGUENESSE. Move was complete at 12.45 pm. Reinforcements of 110 O.R. joined Battn. from draft.	
			1 W.O., 5 Lt. Prior - 2 Lt. Hudson with 11 O.R. from 100th TMB were transferred to 19th TMB. K.K.M. Raley and 16 O.R. were transferred from 100th Bn. Pioneers to 5th Pioneers. Bn. Training. General routine.	
	7.		A + B Coys carried out 7.30 am march to range (Q3.5.B Right) SHEET 51A SE) for musketry practice. Owing to the state of the weather this had to be abandoned by the remainder. Carried out Training. General Routine.	

Army Form C. 2118.

WAR DIARY
INTELLIGENCE SUMMARY.
1st Bn. The Queen's Regt. PAGE 3

FEBRUARY 1918.

(Erase heading not required.)

Date	Hour	Summary of Events and Information	Remarks and references to Appendices
8		2/Lt W. WALLACE and 1 O.R. joined Battn from 3/4 Bn. The Queen's. Training and funeral routine	
9		Capt A.B Ashby and 8 O.R. joined Battn from 3/4 Bn. The Queen's. The battn. carried out range practices on 'C' range. Lewis gunners fired their guns at 300*	
10		The Battn. paraded for Divine service which was held in R.F.C. Concert Hall at 11.15 am. The service was conducted by Rev. O'Rourke who was, previous to the war, chaplain at BORDON during the time the Battn. was stationed there.	
11		The Battn. carried out rapid firing practice at 150* range at Xq 2.2. Training and funeral routine	

WAR DIARY

INTELLIGENCE SUMMARY

1st Bn. THE QUEEN'S

FEBRUARY 1918

PAGE 4

Place	Date	Hour	Summary of Events and Information	Remarks and references to Appendices
	12		The battalion marched by companies to C. Coy Range where the first stage of the A.R.A. platoon competition was carried out. Platoon No competition was selected on points to participate in the 2nd Stage.	
	13		Training general routine.	
	14		Training general routine. The 9th Talbot proceeded to England on a 6 months tour of duty. Training general routine	
	15			
	16		The winning platoons of each company in A.R.A. competition marched to C. Range & took part in the 2nd Stage. The platoon selected to represent the Battn. in the 3rd Stage was No 13 Platoon D. Coy. They however did not qualify to represent the Brigade. Training general routine.	

WAR DIARY

INTELLIGENCE SUMMARY. 1st Bn. THE QUEEN'S Regt.

FEBRUARY 1918   Army Form C. 2118.   PAGE 5

Date	Hour	Summary of Events and Information	Remarks
17.		The battalion paraded for Divine Service at 10 a.m. at X 9. b. 2. 8. The service was attended by G.O.C. division who afterwards distributed the following medal ribbons:– Lt. R.O. Parker MC, 2/Lt. T.P. NEWMAN, DCM, Sergt H. RANDALL, DCM, 8470 Sgt. J. Clarke, M.M., 13078 Pte W. BATCHELOR, M.M. 39450 Pte W. LOGAN M.M. 205247 Pte. S. BROCK, M.M. 4008 Pte A. BECKINSOLE MM. 24472 Pte F. GOACHER, BELGIAN CROIX DE GUERRE. In the afternoon a Battalion Sports Meeting was held. More orders received.	
18.		Transport moved in accordance with 19th Infy Bde. orders by road to RENESCURE at 1.15 p.m. Training general routine.	
19.		Transport moved from RENESCURE to STEENVOORDE. Bn. paraded & marched to Bn. parade ground, Notatinghem for arm drill demonstration. This was followed by Coy. close order practice in quick & slow time & adjustment of S.B.R. More orders issued.	

WAR DIARY
INTELLIGENCE SUMMARY

1st Bn. THE QUEEN'S Regt.
FEBRUARY 1918.
PAGE 6.
Army Form C. 2118.

Place	Date	Hour	Summary of Events and Information	Remarks and references to Appendices
	19/a		2/Lt. F. V. Hay proceeded to England for duty with the Machine Gun Corps.	
ST. JEAN CAMP.	20		Battalion moved by road and rail to ST. JEAN CAMP. Move completed at 2.30 p.m. Other ranks Battalion arrived relieved 4th Bn. Yorkshire Regt. in Support on evening of 21st inst. Transport marched from STEENVOORDE to BRANDHOEK.	Batt. Order No. 45.
Support Line D16 b 15 35.	21		Battalion moved into SUPPORT to LEFT Brigade relieving 4th Bn. The Yorkshire Regt. Relief was completed by 6.20 p.m. 1 man was wounded by a spent Anti Aircraft M. G. Bullet before leaving camp.	Battle Order H/6
	22		Battalion was called upon to provide working & carrying parties for RE's on camps & huts for battalions in front line. Behind G. Officer	

WAR DIARY or INTELLIGENCE SUMMARY

FEBRUARY 1918
1st Bn. THE QUEEN'S REGT

Date	Hour	Summary of Events and Information
23.		and 357 O.R. was furnished. Battalion was engaged when working on Corps huts allotted by improving defensive wiring and collecting salvage. Parties furnished consists of 8 Officers and 380 O.Rks. At 11.40pm the SOS went up on the front of the division on our right. This was followed by SOS from W1L1, S1D5 and infant battalion HQ. 9th T.O.S. as Battn HQ. was thus fired at complete chain. Our barrage came down in 15 seconds. Both Artilley eng. One O.R. wounded – shell.
24		At 12.35am fire slacked very appreciably and finally died away. Enemy shown unusef of the night was quiet. Working parties as usual

FEBRUARY 1918

PAGE 8

Army Form C. 2118.

WAR DIARY or INTELLIGENCE SUMMARY. 1st Bn The QUEEN'S REGT

(Erase heading not required.)

Place	Date	Hour	Summary of Events and Information	Remarks and references to Appendices
			Further detailing Officers and 135 ORs to Brigade orders for relief received. Bn orders for relief issued.	B.O. No 7
	25		Proceeded in company areas and thoroughly cleaned up during morning and afternoon and railway collected. Working parties of 2 Offrs & 60 ORs furnished during morning. Relief commenced to arrive at 5:0pm. Relief was complete at 6:40pm. Battalion marched to ST JEAN CAMP on relief. Everyone busied directly men arrived in Camp.	
ST JEAN CAMP.	26		The Battalion paraded at 8am and marched to new area, allotted for work on Army defence zone. Zone turned work	

WAR DIARY
INTELLIGENCE SUMMARY.
1/3 Bn. The Queen's Regt.

FEBRUARY 1918   Army Form C. 2118.

Place	Date	Hour	Summary of Events and Information	Remarks and references to Appendices
	27		with an hours rest was done before battalion returned to Camp.	
			The battalion spent the morning cleaning up - inspection & baths for remaining men conducted. Baths were allotted during afternoon at YPRES. O's Coys taken over from this battalion in next turn recommended there after dark. One O.R. wounded - shell.	
	28		The battalion spent morning arranging first aid kits in TRENCH DEPOT HUT Battalion inspection were carried out. - Bn order to move into the left front subsector received. O's C. sepp't Coys and 1/9 9/40 reconnoitres support positions.	

F.W.R. Gliddon Lieut Col
Comdg 1/3 Bn The Queen's Regt.

WAR DIARY
INTELLIGENCE SUMMARY
(Erase heading not required.)

MARCH 1918 — 1st Bn The Queen's Regt

Army Form C. 2118.

Place	Date	Hour	Summary of Events and Information	Remarks and references to Appendices
	12.		Relief was complete 4/10.45pm. Batt order to relay men from H.6 Dug received. 10 another 1 O.R killed & O.R wounded.	
			Lt.Col. St.B.R. SLADEN was killed about 10am. by a shell on HEINE HOUSE trench which fell around him. Enemy reply to our incoming fire continued with increasing [illegible] [illegible] T.M's fire against our post was maintained throughout the afternoon. Our posts & our observation shots which gave us then considerably. Situation Normal.	
	13.		At 12 midnight a fighting patrol of Mr W.J.A MORGAN Mr W O.R, C Coy, went out to reconnoitre GASOMETERS. Had still a M.O. fire from three out to move danger & posn enemy obtained investigation. They came to within 15yds of the GASOMETERS & lay still. Except for movement	

WAR DIARY
INTELLIGENCE SUMMARY.

MARCH 1918

Army Form C. 2118.

1/3rd Middlesex Regt. Page 6.

Place	Date	Hour	Summary of Events and Information	Remarks and references to Appendices
			At 9th the enemy were seen to enter the Trenches & a machine gun was observed firing from our flank. Our forward moved Vis-à-Vis with this situation and wounded the I.O.S. men in up to this. Lieut. Rth. Batm. to investigate. Left with the wealth that 6th hand commenced firing on and around Graevetine the Patrol then withdrew any causes. Our casualties was 2 O.R. wounded.	
	14		Lieutenant named T/: WAT MORGAN and party of 8 O.R. went out on fighting patrol at 12 midnight. A short distance ahead our posts they observed a large party of the enemy. Thirty or about twenty-five they attacked without a collision was held then not far then then they hop forward. With the highest casualties 1 O.R. killed 2 wounded	

MARCH 1918 — 1st Bn. The Queen's Regt. — PAGE 6

WAR DIARY or INTELLIGENCE SUMMARY
(Erase heading not required.)

Place	Date	Hour	Summary of Events and Information	Remarks and references to Appendices
	15		Enemy artillery activity on our front was above normal. About 12.15am our artillery acted & fired the barrage from a prisoner captured at 2 a.m. the previous morning it was confirmed. It fire & lost lives at 4 stores both officers. News of an enemy artillery raid was received from 1/8th R. & 1/4th Bn. to put the companies at 9.2.50 a.m. At 1 a.m. enemy opened heavy artillery fire T.M. barrage on our front & a part field every about 30 along our whole front. There was observed approximately No. 3 pts left front bay (on Q) think enemy was seen to run. Then from our rifle & L.G. fire, No 3 & 5 M.G. at the morning with rifle at L.G. fire. Other N.O. 3 in consolidated at heavy OG dobris in disorder. The enemy lost at least 90 of his enemy in intercepted wires & prisoners 3 pots by 30 a.m. At 2 a.m. situation was normal again. Owing to the ground failure to reach in any line from in &	

WAR DIARY
INTELLIGENCE SUMMARY. 1st Bn. The Queens Regt.

MARCH 1918   Army Form C. 2118.
PAGE 7

Place	Date	Hour	Summary of Events and Information	Remarks and references to Appendices
			small parties attached to own platoons probably worked prisoners showing knowledge of the line over which they [?] hay-book and [?] papers [?] [?] to delegate to the 5th Bn 6th Rgt. Bn also [?] for relief received a [?] under 2nd K of [?] moved in to Police Bath. commence at 7.45 pm. Relief was completed at 10.10pm. On reliefs being [?] to [?] to BORRY Fm when Bus [?] [?] a cheval provided to ST JEAN CAMP. Each [?] reached there [?] on arrival at camp.	80, 60
ST JEAN CAMP	16		Remaining up to the [?] orders.	
	17		Working parties of H.M + 155 OR. were furnished to [?] [?] in cleaning Corduroy Camp and cleaning up equipment etc.	

WAR DIARY or INTELLIGENCE SUMMARY

Army Form C. 2118.

1st/5th "THE QUEEN'S" Regt.   MARCH 1918

Place	Date	Hour	Summary of Events and Information	Remarks and references to Appendices
ST JEAN CAMP	18th		Battalion employed on working parties under R.E. in Battle Area. Camp was shelled intermittently from 4 am to 10 pm from the N.E. and S. No casualties. Battn. Diary & memo to BRANDHOEK as usual.	
TORONTO CAMP	19th		Bn. shelter march to TORONTO CAMP. No casualties. Ranges etc used for work out with the R.E's. & by the men for company training. Hostile shelled round in TORONTO Camp. Work & wiring marches back from the lines other ranks to ST JEAN Bank. Map tables showing the men to march to BRANDHOEK. Workers whilst by 3:15 pm Bn. arrives & are restricted to bivouac 2/A.V.S.H. received. 7/h 2/M Aircraft Inc proceed to England Immediately.	
	20th		General Routine followed 1st line of Battalion without halt. Bn. H.Q. at IRKSOME (near HAMBURG) in relief of 2nd/4th 2nd/A.S.H. in morning. 2 ps not secured. Battalion moved trench for treatment. 5/l.l. knot injured from hostile Artillery fire received	

WAR DIARY or INTELLIGENCE SUMMARY

1st Bn. The Queens Regt.

MARCH 1918.

Army Form C. 2118.

Place	Date	Hour	Summary of Events and Information	Remarks and references to Appendices
CONTD CAMP	20th		that LtCol N. KEMP WELCH DSO MC has been appointed to the command of the Battalion.	
	21st		Battalion marched at 4.15am and entrained by lt Railway Station BRANDHOEK in two trains at 5am and 5.15am respectively. Detrained at BORRE FARM at 6.50am and proceeded by platoon at 1 min intervals to Entrench Sys not head of HAMBURG. No very great delay in being put interdependent on return to platoon. S.B. Ro med situation during a Company held from LEVI COTTS after which the next Company held trained & relief proceeded to the Relief was completed at 9.10am Coys being distributed as follows – WATERFIELDS "B" Coy LEFT CENTRE "B" Coy – RIGHT CENTRE "A" Coy – RIGHT "D" Coy. A, B & D Coys are situated at at HAMBURG. Intermittent shelling during day including a number of gas shells	

Army Form C. 2118.

Page 10.

WAR DIARY
INTELLIGENCE SUMMARY

(Erase heading not required.)

1/6 Bn "The Queens" Regt

MARCH 1918

Place	Date	Hour	Summary of Events and Information	Remarks and references to Appendices
2KSQ1E	21st		Casualties 1 Butcher. 3 O.R. wounded during shelling of YPRES.	
	22nd		Night 21st/22nd. Hostile aircraft that a heavy afternoon was carried out by the Gifford Battery between 3am and 2.30 am, for which heavy retaliation was resp. by the Day normal. 2/Lt W. WALLACE proceeded to England with orders to report to O.C. R.F.C. with view to employment with that Corps. 2/Lt W. EHEN proceeded to England for transfer to the Indian Army. Memo from G.H.Q. in which 29 warrant officers & n.c.o's the Cn for in Catine of the Corps Commander is forwarded with reference to enemy raids 2 O.R. killed 1 O.R. wounded in back over shelling in YPRES district.	Vin copies Memo attd.

WAR DIARY
INTELLIGENCE SUMMARY

MARCH 1918 Army Form C. 2118.
1st Bn. The Queen's R[egt].

Place	Date	Hour	Summary of Events and Information	Remarks
IRKSOME 23			Enemy quiet during morning. At 1.50pm artillery area shoot was commenced on WATERFIELDS lasting until about 5pm. During this period some 300 shells were thrown into the locality. There were no casualties. The enemy's working & carrying parties were punished. 2/Lieut C.H. WATT was S.O.S from this date. 3. Company sniping opened upon enemy cable parties under supervision of Div. Signal Officer from 7am to 8am. Whether normal a quiet day. The usual sniping & carrying parties punished. About 6.15pm 2 F.A. appeared over our forward gun lines but although heavily fired on were not apparently damaged. At the rear of these M.G. were our about 2500 feet down on SKINE area. Although several enemy parties were in the vicinity there were no casualties.	118

WAR DIARY

MARCH 1918.

INTELLIGENCE SUMMARY. 1st Bn. The Queen's Regt.

PAGE 12

Place	Date	Hour	Summary of Events and Information	Remarks and references to Appendices
IRKSOME	25th		Lieut. Col. M. KEMP-WELCH, D.S.O., M.C. joined Battalion and assumed command. Relief was normal & minor operations were carried out on the front of the left battalion of the upper division. Enemy retaken and not used on front. Hostile shelly of SEINE area at 8.15pm to 6.45 p.m. No casualties. B.O. 66 under 2nd Inf. Bn.	B.O. 66
	26th		Bn. orders for relief issued. Enemy was active firing on SEINE - HAMBURG & WATERFIELDS area during morning. Enemy attempted to raise up post of B Brigade Front held by "C" Company and was repulsed. On artillery fire in response to the S.O.S. signal. The S.O.S. was also fired on front of night brigade left division. Bn. order 69 Casualties 1 O.R. Killed 2 O.R. wounded.	B.O. 69
	27th		Bn. was relieved by 4th Bn. The Kings. Relief was completed by	

WAR DIARY

MARCH 1918 Army Form C. 2118.
1st Bn. The Queens Regt PAGE 13

Place	Date	Hour	Summary of Events and Information	Remarks and references to Appendices
ST. LAWRENCE CAMP	27	8.15 a.m.	Bn less C Coy then proceeded to POPPY Fm & thence by lyl. railway to BRANDHOEK marching to ST LAWRENCE CAMP. Move was completed by 10.10 a.m. C Coy on completion of work marched to WIELTJE Rwy frog station & proceeded by train to BRANDHOEK. Thence marched to Camp reaching Camp by 4.0 p.m. Baths were allotted to Bn & the men except by by Battns. after dinner. Seven N.C.O's Men & Others changing up of kits & men proceeded M.M. by the Corps Commander.	See Attached Authority.
	28.		A, B & D Coys proceeded to DIVISIONAL RESERVE AMMUNITION ROUND from 9 a.m. whereas C Coy was engaged in cleaning up kits & Inspection were held	
	29		A & B Coys proceeded to Army Baths by bus for work on wire. C & D were employed in cleaning kits inspection & General Training. Baths were allotted to C Coy.	

WAR DIARY
INTELLIGENCE SUMMARY: 1st Bn. The Queens Regt.

MARCH 1918   Army Form C. 2118.
PAGE 14

Place	Date	Hour	Summary of Events and Information	Remarks and references to Appendices
ST LAWRENCE CAMP.	30.		Training and general routine. Football was played in the afternoon.	
	31		Battalion paraded at 9.45am for Divine Service which was held in Recreation hut in Camp. The C.O. No's C Coy reconnoitred the right Brigade sub-sector of the Divisional Front. Bde. order received for move by bus to LIENCOURT An- at 1 pm. Battalion paraded at 5.15pm and marched to entraining point G.6.D.4.3. Battalion entrained at 8pm moved off at 9pm. Transport moved by road under orders O.C. No 3 Coy. Train ASC.	

W Temple Welch.
Lieut Colonel.
Comdg 1st Bn The Queens Regt.

19th Brigade.

33rd Division.

1st BATTALION

THE QUEEN'S (Royal West Surrey) REGIMENT

APRIL 1918.

Report on Operations, Operation Orders & Maps under separate cover.

WAR DIARY
INTELLIGENCE SUMMARY
(Erase heading not required.)

Army Form C. 2118.

APRIL 1918   2/6 Bn. "THE QUEEN'S" Regt.

Place	Date	Hour	Summary of Events and Information	Remarks and references to Appendices
	1		Move proceeded with Battalion debussing at HENCOURT and marching to BEAUFORT where accommodation was provided. Move was completed by 8 a.m. Transport completed 1st days trek at 3 a.m. halting at MORBECQUE. At 9 a.m. Transport resumed march & billeted at MARLES LES MINES at 4 p.m. Battalion transferred under orders to 2/6/12.	
	2		Training general nature. Ran a a-side platoon tournament was played in the afternoon. The Transport resumed march at 9 a.m. and arrived at BEAUFORT at 6 p.m.	
	3		Training and general routine. A Staff ride, under Brigade arrangements, was held in the afternoon, all mounted officers attending.	

WAR DIARY
INTELLIGENCE SUMMARY.

1st Bn. The Queen's Regt. Army Form C. 2118.

APRIL 1918

PAGE 2

Place	Date	Hour	Summary of Events and Information	Remarks and references to Appendices
	4.		Training general routine	
	5		Warning order to move received from Brigade. 8.30 am Battalion paraded at 9.45 a.m. Battalion paraded at 11.30 am and marched to battalion starting point on MAROEUIL BEAUFORT - AVESNES Rd. Rear of the B in BEAUFORT. The Battalion then moved via AVESNES-LE-COMTE - LATTRE ST QUENTIN - NOYELLETTE - HABARCQ - LARESSET to DUISANS area the battalion being accommodated in Nissen & Moiseros Huts at 3.40 p.m.	BO. No. 79
Y Camp	6.		Training and general routine. Bn. training order to move received. Bn. orders for move to BEAUFORT issued. Battalion Orders issued.	
DUISANS				BO No 80
	7		Battalion paraded at 9.45 a.m. and march marched to BEAUFORT. Move was completed by 11.50 A.M. Lieut J.A. DICKINSON joined Battn.	

WAR DIARY
INTELLIGENCE SUMMARY.
1st Bn. The Queen's Regt.

APRIL 1918 Army Form C. 2118.
PAGE 3

Place	Date	Hour	Summary of Events and Information	Remarks and references to Appendices
BEAUFORT	8		Training of general routine	
	9		Training of general routine. Haig's "Backs-to-the-Wall" Special Order of the Day was read to all Ranks. The Battalion winners lectured on the Battle.	
	10		Training of general routine. At 1.40 pm orders were received for Battalion to be ready to move at 2 hours notice. At 5 pm orders were received to be prepared to move by tactical train at 1 hour's notice. Transport by road. Ammunition on the man to be made up to 170 rounds. At 7.30 pm Bde order moves for move to entrain. Battalion marched off at 8.30 pm an proceeded to AUBIGNY station via AVESNES-LE-COMTE - HAMEAU - TILLOY-LES-HERMAVILLE, where entrainment was carried out. Bookers, water carts was cut. Accompanied the Battalion Transport left AUBIGNY at 3.15 AM. The train arrived at CAESTRE at 2 pm.	
	11			

WAR DIARY / INTELLIGENCE SUMMARY

(Erase heading not required.)

Army Form C. 2118.
PAGE 4.

1st Bn. The Queen's Regt.
APRIL 1918

Place	Date	Hour	Summary of Events and Information	Remarks and references to Appendices
METEREN	11		Retirement was carried out immediately. Battalion was conveyed by bus to METEREN where it remained in bivouac. The Brigade was in Corps Reserve & prepared to move at short notice. Fighting order was prepared and ammunition made up to 220 rounds per man. Piquets were posted on the avenues of approach to the village & he held against surprise. Intermittent shelling of the ridge took place during the night. 1 OR wounded.	
	12	At 11.30 AM	Warning order received to be prepared to move at 10 minutes notice. Wilpen Baroulier was ordered to move out and take up positions S. of METEREN. Rapid & the village. This was done – battalion was clear of bivouac in 15 minutes. Troops in their fighting positions by 3.15 pm and touch with the enemy obtained by screen of battle patrols followed to attached	Appendix I–II

WAR DIARY
INTELLIGENCE SUMMARY.
1st Bn. The Queen's Regt.

APRIL 1918

PAGE 5

Army Form C. 2118.

Place	Date	Hour	Summary of Events and Information	Remarks and references to Appendices
METEREN	12		A shell fell in the camp as the battalion was parading to move off. Killed H.F.D. FAULKNER and 8 O.R. wounded.	
	13		The transport completed the move from BEAUPORT arriving in the NOOTE BOOM area at 6 a.m. B.Echelon lines then established.	
	14		The battalion on relief marched to the NOOTE BOOM area. The four companies arriving at 11.50 p.m. The whole battalion in detailo 31st to the division attached to new billets by 5.30 a.m. The day was given over to not so cleaning up. The battalion was notified that they were under short notice to move.	B.O. 81
NOOTE BOOM	15			
	16		At 10 a.m. orders were received to march to above as enemy had forced passage of SE corner of METEREN. as	

WAR DIARY
INTELLIGENCE SUMMARY

APRIL 1918   Army Form C. 2118.

1st Bn. The Queen's Regt.

Date	Hour	Summary of Events and Information	Remarks and references to Appendices
16	10.15 AM	Orders were received from Division to occupy "Blue line" from S end of wood in R.32.a to Rouge Park in R.27.c inclusive. 33rd Composite Unit held from left of Bn. to crossroads in R.28.d. A coy of XXII Corps Cyclists were also placed under the orders of the C.O. Battalion HQ was established at R.26.d.2.5. The CO established a further command at R.27.a.25.95. The transport minimum reserve marched to BOESCHEPE where they bivouaced.	Ref. 2/55 20000
		6 OR wounded	
17	At 11.45 AM orders were received from 32 Divn that the 33rd Divn. Composite Unit & XXII Corps Cyclists went withdrawn from "Blue" line leaving the battalion alone on the reserve line. 3 wounded 2 missing. 1 OR killed	
18	At 2.15 pm Bn orders were received known with line	

WAR DIARY of INTELLIGENCE SUMMARY

APRIL 1918. 1st Bn The Queen's Regt.

Army Form C. 2118. PAGE 7.

Place	Date	Hour	Summary of Events and Information	Remarks and references to Appendices
	18		Taking over from X 20 Central 5 x 14 d. Thereunder reserve was rejoined the battalion. At 3.30 p.m. orders were rec'd the Bn. was cancelled. Bn was withdrawn more into the Blue Line & disposed in forms against further positions. The men were given what rest and what sleep. Bde. order received for Battalion to kindly know 1/2 an hour notice to support 34" Division receiving Bn. in order to move off at 4 a.m. to R.29.B. where they were to remain till night 19th/20th.	
	19.		Battn. moved off at 4.30 a.m. & marched to R.29.B. where they were placed under the shelter of huge & took under orders to move up. Each man dug a shelter for shell splinters. Orders received from Bde. to take over line from S.7.b.3.7 & S.1.a.8.5. This order was	

WAR DIARY

INTELLIGENCE SUMMARY

1st Bn. The Queens Regt.

APRIL 1918   Army Form C. 2118.
PAGE 8

Place	Date	Hour	Summary of Events and Information	Remarks and references to Appendices
	19		Subsequently amended to read "Reserve line from X 11 B 88 to St JAN'S CAPEL Rn (X 6 Central) further "Duke of Wellington's" Battalion orders issued. Battalion moved off at 11 pm. Relief was complete at 12.30 am. Tarandellies 1 Offr. & 11 OR. arrived. Bn H.Q. was established in the Convent R 36.0. 60	S.O. No 83
St JAN'S CAPEL	20		Bde order received for relief by 1/32nd French Regt. on this 20/21st. Battalion orders issued. As the position held by the Battalion was not taken over the Moordin had to wait until 55th Divn relieved	S.O. No 84
	21		Battalion was relieved at 3 am. on relief moved to own billets even at O.23.D. where billets not being issued. Thence chapel orders noted. Thence marched at 9.20 am the Battalion marched to another via P 25 c 9.7 via EECKE - St SYLVESTRE CAPEL - KOORTEN KOOP MOLR was complete by 2.30 pm	

WAR DIARY
INTELLIGENCE SUMMARY.

APRIL 1918 1st Bn The Queen's Regt
PAGE 9.

Place	Date	Hour	Summary of Events and Information	Remarks and references to Appendices
CAMPAGNE	22		The Battalion was bathed & clean clothes being worn in bath houses in the Camps. Reinforcements of 103 O.R. joined Battalion. Training general routine.	
DRAVE	23	at 9am	The Battalion has A D Coys paraded in mass were inspected by Major Gen R.J. PINNEY, CB. The G.O.C. addressed the Battalion upon their magnificent stand during the period 12-14" inst. and stated that the large amount of credit given to the Division during the fighting above INKSTEREN was entirely due to the Battalion's splendid braveries fully the days in one line and preventing the enemy from breaking through though it entails the excess losses a general routine were carried out	
	24		Training general routine.	

WAR DIARY
INTELLIGENCE SUMMARY.
1st Bn The Queens Regt

APRIL 1918

Army Form C. 2118.

PAGE 10

Place	Date	Hour	Summary of Events and Information	Remarks and references to Appendices
	25		Training general routine. Capt. T.R. HARMER, The Middlesex Regt joined Battalion today.	
	26		Battalion received warning order from Bde to be ready to move at short notice. Trouble in vicinity of camp carried out.	
	27.		Training general routine	
	28.		The Battalion paraded at 10.10 AM and marched to Brigade parade ground which was held in a hangar of the aerodrome. 2nd Lieut C. JACKSON joined Battalion from 3rd Battalion. Warning order for move to ROCQUIGNY	
	29			R.O. 95

WAR DIARY
or
INTELLIGENCE SUMMARY.
(Erase heading not required.)

Army Form C. 2118.

PAGE 11.

APRIL 1918

Place	Date	Hour	Summary of Events and Information	Remarks and references to Appendices
CAMPAGNE	29		[illegible]	
BREV.			[illegible]	
			Made back to Camp [illegible]	
			[illegible]	
			[illegible]	
			and Shower baths at 9 pm	
	30		Training general routine. 2/Lts. J. S. ROBINSON, W. J. PRATT, F. L. HARTLEY, H. B. ROE, E. H. HAMMOND, R. W. DAVIS, A. H. CHILCOTT, A. G. TELLING, C. A. WATTS joined the Battalion from East Surrey Regt. in England.	

W Kemp Welch Lt Col Regt.
Comdg. 1st Bn. The Queen's

19th Brigade.
33rd Division.

WAR DIARY & APPENDICES.

1st BATTALION

THE QUEEN'S ROYAL WEST SURREY REGIMENT

APRIL 1918.

APPENDIX I

AWARDS

BAR TO MILITARY CROSS	Capt. G.F. ASHPITAL. M.C.
MILITARY CROSS	Capt. H.A. NORTH.
	Awarded by Army Commander.
	(Authy 3rd Army R.O. 1891 O/- 3/1/18)
" "	Lieut C.S. CLARK.
	J. RUDKIN.
	H.C. CRAWLEY.
	Awarded by Army Commander
	(Authy 3rd Army R.O. 1876 O/- 20/1/18)
DISTINGUISHED CONDUCT MEDAL	No 9439 Sgt D.R. AYLING
	Awarded by Army Commander.
	(Authy 3rd Army R.O. 1891 O/- 3/1/18)
BAR TO MILITARY MEDAL	No 205247 Pte S. BROCK.
MILITARY MEDAL	No 30452 Cpl. J. MURPHY.
	206024 " G. JOHNSON.
	6795 Pte S.H. SMITH
	Awarded by Corps Commander.
	(Authy V Corps R.O. No 982 O/- 2/1/18)
" "	No 10620 Pte A. PRIME.
	11659 Sgt H.G. PULLEN.
	6829 Pte W. MARKWORTH.
	Awarded by Corps Commander
	(Authy V Corps R.O. No 985 O/- 4/1/18.

Certified True Extracts

J. Thipton /Lt
a/Adj 1st Bn The Queen's Regt.

STANDING ORDERS FOR MOVE.

The following orders will be strictly observed throughout the move unless otherwise stated in Battalion Orders.

1. All steel helmets and box respirators will not be unused until after the conclusion of the move.

2. Blankets will be rolled in tens, securely tied in 3 places, and clearly labelled. They will be collected daily as under, at times to be stated in Battn Orders:-
   1st Journey. Lorry will collect from H.Q "A" & "B" at respective H.Q.
   2nd Journey. Lorry will pick up blankets of "C" and "D" Coys which will be dumped at Q.M. Stores.

3. Jerkins will be carried by Lorry under arrangements to be notified later.

4. Officer's Valises, which must not exceed 65 lbs in weight will be loaded on the Baggage Waggon at Q.M. Stores at a time notified daily in Battn Orders.

5. F.S.M.O. throughout the march will consist of full equipment - greatcoat, mess tin & necessaries IN the pack. Waterproof sheets UNDER the flap of the pack. Caps will on no account be carried outside the pack or haversack.

6. The strictest march discipline will be observed throughout the march particular attention being paid to Bde March Discipline Orders. All officers must be in possession of copies.

7. A billeting party of 1 off and 6 O.Rks will be detailed daily in Battalion Orders. It will consist of the Interpreter + 1 N.C.O (normally C.Q.M.S) per Coy and Bn H.Q. This party will proceed as a party on bicycles in advance of the Battalion. On no a/c will individual men be sent on in advance of the Battn.

8. O's C. Coys will ensure by personal inspection that their billeting area is left in a clean and sanitary condition before moving off. As no party will be left behind, steps must be taken to ensure that this is completed in time.

9. Watches will be synchronised daily at least ½ an hour before Battn Parades. It is the duty of all officers to have the correct time.

10. Standing Trench Orders 33rd Divn para 28 (d) & (e):-
    (d) As soon as a formation or unit arrives in a new area two orderlies will be sent to the Bde Signal Office, one to deliver messages from the Signal Office, the other will return to deliver messages to the Signal Office.
    (e) All runners will be specially instructed as to the position of Bn H.Q. and must be prepared to direct anyone to the quarters occupied.

11. If the Brigade is quartered in wooden huts the greatest care will be taken to ensure that no damage is done to the huts. Severe disciplinary action will be taken against any infringements of this order.

12. Immediately on arrival in billets, O's C. Coys will render falling out state to O. Room.

    Transport 1. One man in addition to the driver is permitted to ride on the box seat of the G.S. waggon. This place will be allotted by the M.O. and the man must be in possession of written authority sgd by him.
    2. Lewis Gun limbers and pack ponies will invariably march with their Coys. Instructions will be issued daily regarding cookers.
    3. A gap of 50 yards will be left behind every group of

12. Vehicles. The last vehicle of each group will be marked with a white disc.

(Sgd) J.E. Shipton Lieut & Adjt.
"The Queen's" Regiment

19th Brigade.

33rd Division.

REPORT ON OPERATIONS Etc.

1st BATTALION "THE QUEEN'S)R.W.Surrey) REGIMENT

APRIL 1918.

WAR DIARY
or
INTELLIGENCE SUMMARY.

(Erase heading not required.)

Army Form C. 2118.

Instructions regarding War Diaries and Intelligence Summaries are contained in F. S. Regs., Part II. and the Staff Manual respectively. Title pages will be prepared in manuscript.

Place	Date	Hour	Summary of Events and Information	Remarks and references to Appendices

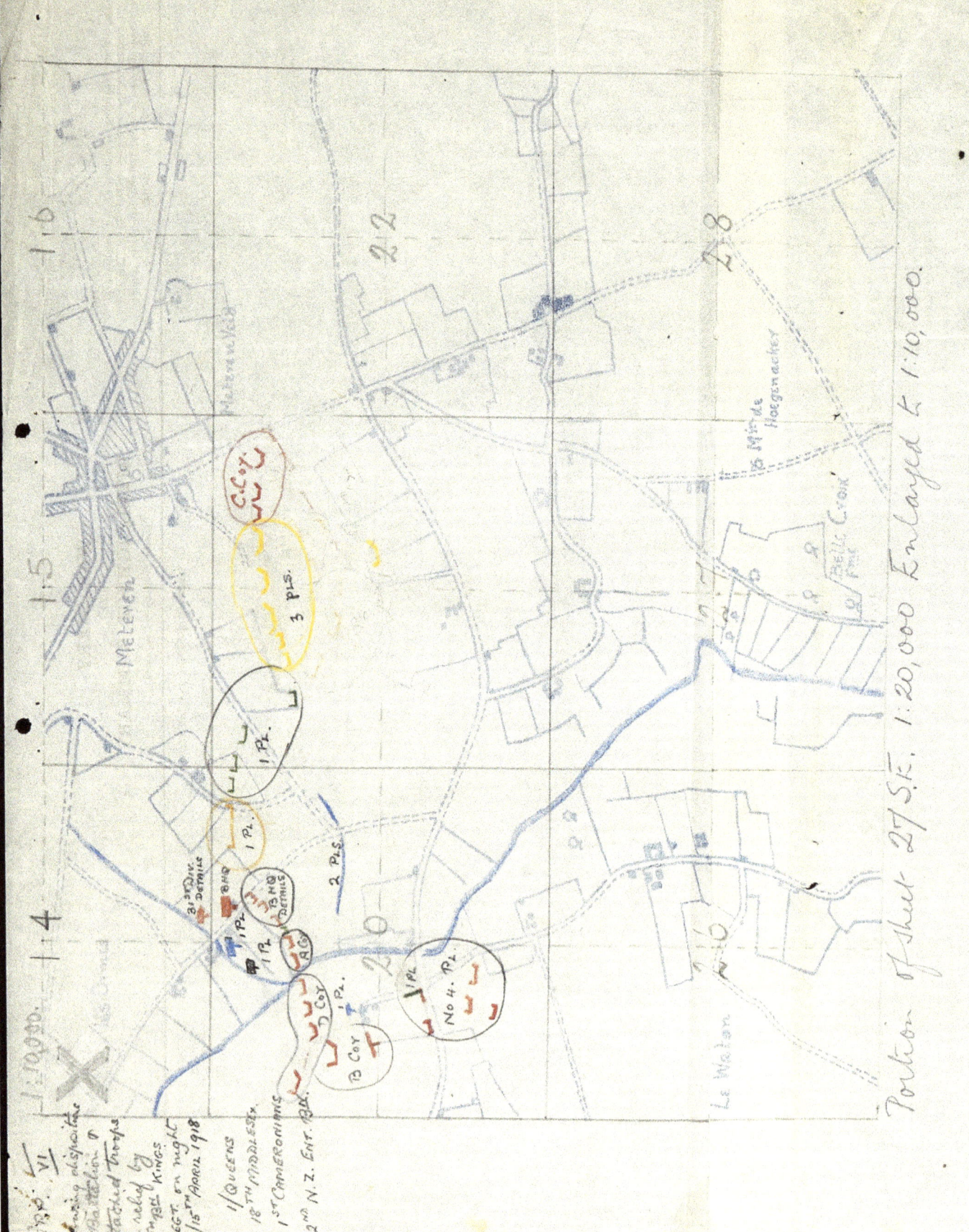

Army Form C. 2118.

WAR DIARY
or
INTELLIGENCE SUMMARY.
(Erase heading not required.)

Instructions regarding War Diaries and Intelligence Summaries are contained in F. S. Regs., Part II. and the Staff Manual respectively. Title pages will be prepared in manuscript.

Place	Date	Hour	Summary of Events and Information	Remarks and references to Appendices

(A8201) Wt W1771/M2031 750,000 5/17 Sch. 52 Forms/C2118/14 D. D. & L., London, E.C.

Army Form C. 2118.

WAR DIARY
or
INTELLIGENCE SUMMARY.

(Erase heading not required.)

Place	Date	Hour	Summary of Events and Information	Remarks and references to Appendices

Instructions regarding War Diaries and Intelligence Summaries are contained in F. S. Regs., Part II. and the Staff Manual respectively. Title pages will be prepared in manuscript.

(A8co4) D. D. & L., London, E.C. Wt W1771/M2031 750,000 5/17 **Sch. 58** Forms/C2118/14

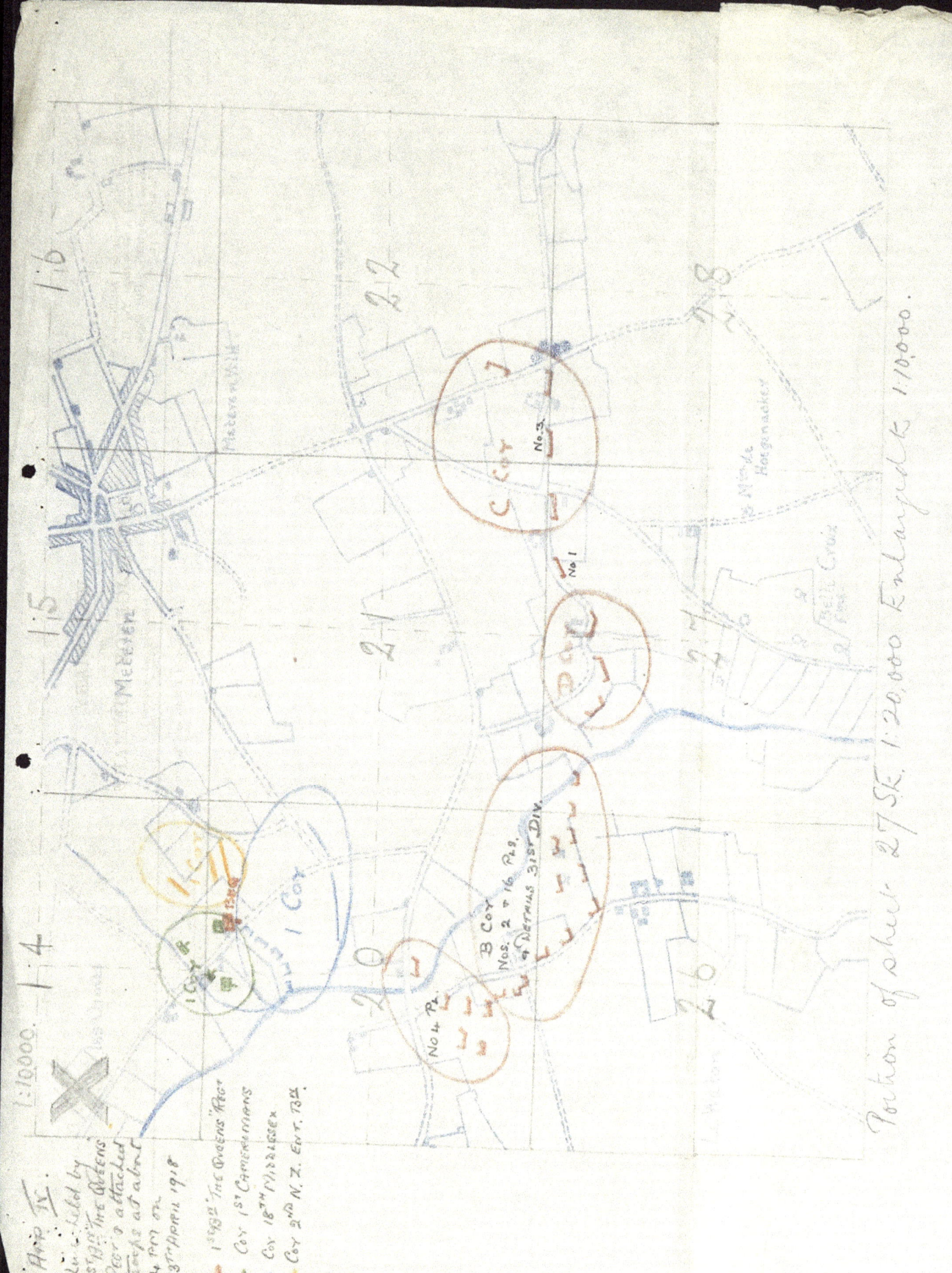

Army Form C. 2118.

WAR DIARY
or
INTELLIGENCE SUMMARY.

(Erase heading not required.)

Place	Date	Hour	Summary of Events and Information	Remarks and references to Appendices

Instructions regarding War Diaries and Intelligence Summaries are contained in F. S. Regs., Part II. and the Staff Manual respectively. Title pages will be prepared in manuscript.

(A8co1) D. D. & L., London, E.C. W† W1771/M2031 750,000 5/17 **Sch. 52** Forms/C2118/14

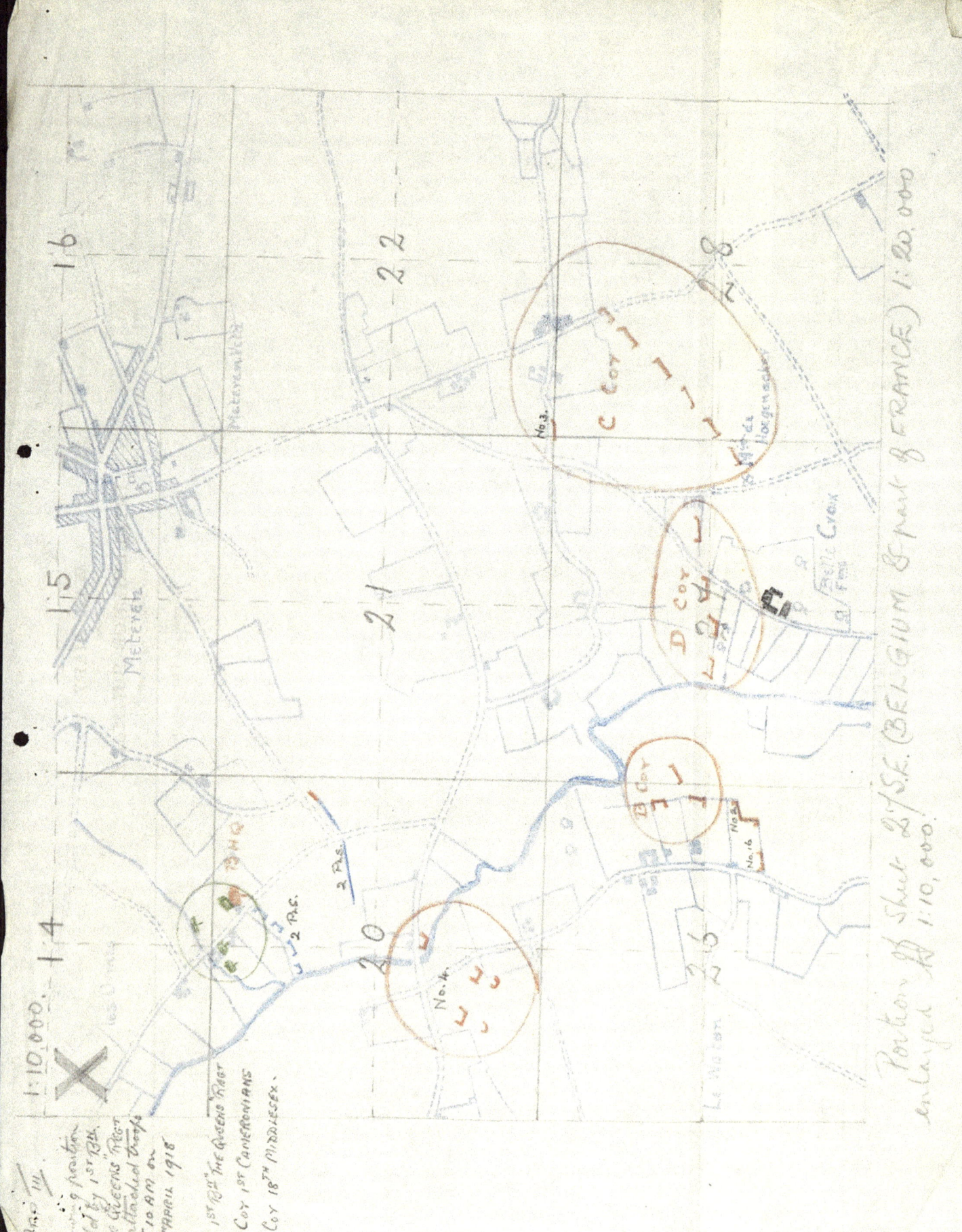

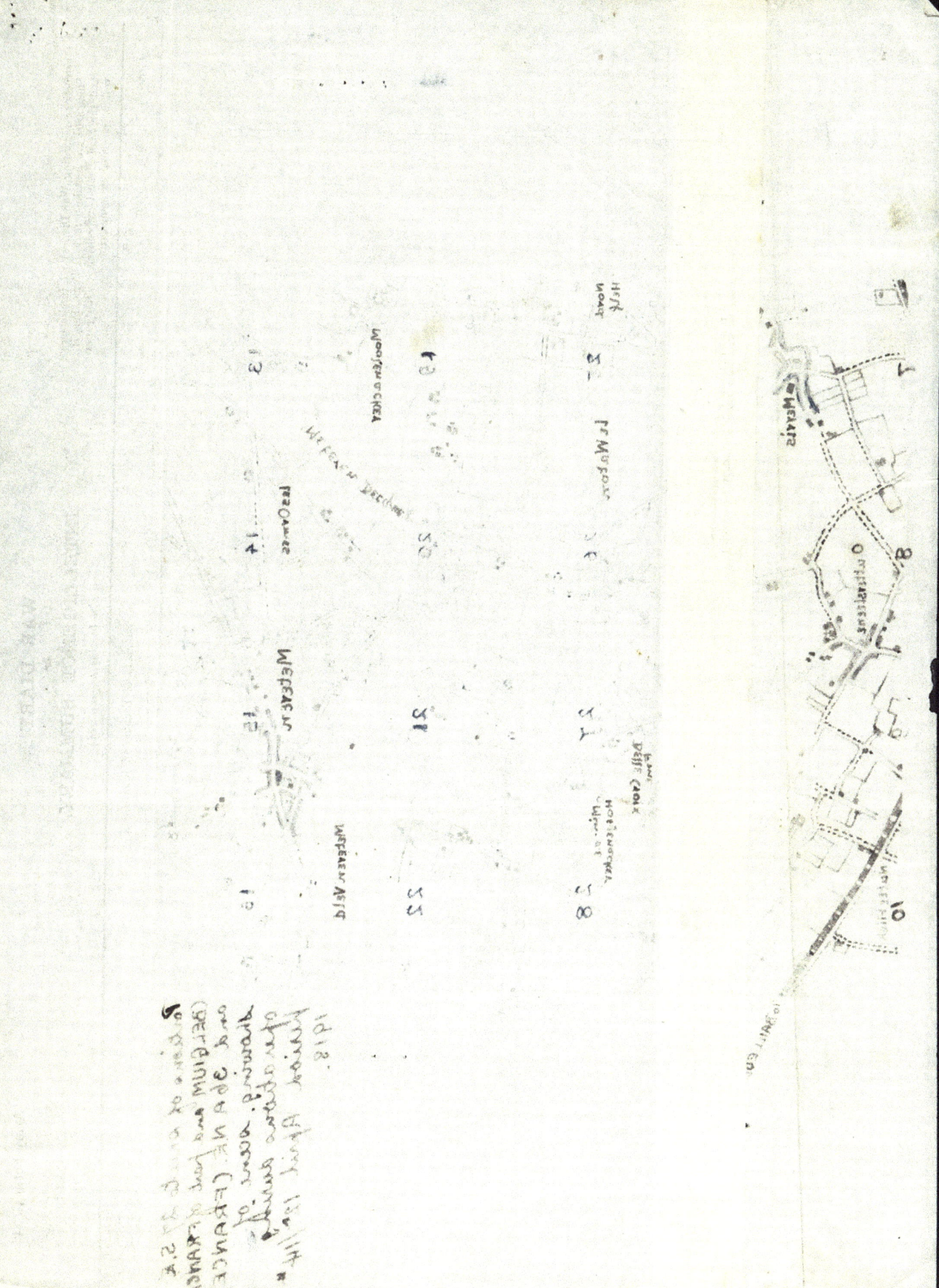

WAR DIARY
or
INTELLIGENCE SUMMARY.
(Erase heading not required.)

Army Form C. 2118.

APRIL 1918

Appendix II

1/4 Bn. The Queen's Regt.

Place	Date	Hour	Summary of Events and Information	Remarks and references to Appendices
	App II		Showing in red, positions taken up by 1st Bn. The Queen's Regt on afternoon of 12th April 1918.	Portions of sheets 27 S.E. (BELGIUM and part of FRANCE) and 36A N.E. (FRANCE) showing scene of operations during period April 12th/14th 1918.

OPERATIONS SOUTH OF METEREN 12-14/April/1918.

Battalion under Command Lt.Col.M.Kemp-Welch, D.S.O., M.C.,

At Battalion Headquarters Major H.E.Ironmonger.
Capt.& Adjt.R.H.Nevins.
Lt.K.M.East.
2/Lt.P.Jakes.

With No.1.Company.
Capt.H.J.Carpenter Lieut G.F.A.S.OPITEL.
2/Lt.L.O.Parkes,M.C.
2/Lt.C.W.Elliott.
2/Lt.H.G.Sweet.

With No.2.Company.
Capt.A.M.Allan.
Lieut.I.T.P.Hughes.
2/Lt.T.Crompton.
2/Lt.E.de W.Green.

With No.3.Company.
Capt.H.Ribton-Cooke M.C
Lieut.H.Mallett.
Lieut.G.Stevenson.
2/Lt.R.J.Brooks.
2/Lt.F.Russen.

With No.4.Company.
Capt.N.D.Avery.
Lieut.J.A.Dickinson.
2/Lt.J.E.Corry.
2/Lt.H.B.Donny.
Medical Officer. (Capt.E.C.Gayner)
M.C,R.A.M.C.

Reference Map $\frac{1}{20,000}$ Sheet 27 S.E.

12th April. On the night 11/12th April, the Battalion was close billeted in huts at West end of METEREN, X.15.c.9.9. The village was shelled continuously during the night, but only one casualty was incurred by the Battalion although crowded in a dangerous locality. The Battalion was held in readiness to move at very short notice.

1 p.m. Commanding Officer was sent for to Brigade Headquarters at Map reference X.c.9.7. and Battalion was ordered to fall in. C.O. received written orders original of which is attached as appendix (1) ordering Battalion to occupy a defensive position at once, covering METEREN, in squares X.20.c.- 21.c.- 21.d.- 22.c.- 22.d. a distance of 3000 yards as 31st Division was reported to be retiring northwards in direction of this place.

Very short verbal orders were issued to assembled Company Commanders. B.C.& D.Companies were ordered to occupy this front, approximate Company frontages being given. Commanding Officer was to have selected line and adjusted Company frontages on the ground. A Company, Battalion Reserve, was ordered to assemble about X.20.b. Farm at X.15. c. o.2. was provisionally selected as Battalion Headquarters. While orders were being issued a shell fell in Camp and wounded Lieut.H.F.D.Faulker and eight other ranks.

1-15 p.m. Companies move out, approximately 15 minutes after receipt of Brigade Orders by Commanding Officer, C. along METEREN - X.27, B.& D. along X.15 a. X.20.B. road.

2.

1-30 p.m. Commanding Officer riding forward met Brigade Commander at X.20.d.7.6. and was told that Brigade Commander had ordered C.Company to occupy high ground further south with Company right at MOULIN - DE - HOEGENACKER - X.27.d.2.8. and that remainder of Battalion was to be deployed on this line facing East-South East. C.Company (Capt.H.R.Ribton-Cook,M.C.) had already moved forward to this new objective B.Company (Capt.A.M.Allan) and D.Company (Capt.N.B.Avery) were met on the road and ordered to occupy line, D.Company HILL X.27.d.8.8. to South end of enclosure X.27.d.1.2., B.Company to prolong this line to South-west.

1-45 p.m. The high ground that the Battalion was to occupy was found to be held by enemy machine guns. These however inflicted very few casualties during the advance which was carried out in an extremely quick and efficient manner, through some intricate and enclosed country.

2 p.m. C.Company moving into position encountered machine gun at HILL. This was immediately engaged and captured by 2/Lt.F.RUSSEN and 8 men. The Company then took up its position (See map appendix 2) and dug in with entrenching tools as no tools were available when Battalion moved off.

D.Company reached its objective at about the same time without much opposition and dug in as shown on map (appendix 2)

2-30 p.m. B.Company moving on to the ridge SOUTH OF BELLE CROIX FARM encountered enemy machine gun and riflemen in enclosures in F.3.a & b. These were never satisfactorily dealt with owing to the length of front which the Company had to occupy. The party of about 50 other ranks mostly belonging to the 11th Bn. East Yorkshire Regt.were collected under Command of 2/Lt.DIMOND 11th East Yorks and came under Command of O.C.B.Company.

2-45 p.m. Commanding Officer reconnoitred along road X.20 central - F.2.d. and found no formed body of our troops on or behind the Battalion's right flank. He decided that it was inadvisable to leave a flank in the air between BELLE CROIX FARM and OUTTERSTEENE until there was some certainty of other troops becoming available to prolong or protect the Battalion's right flank. The right of 'B' Company was therefore bent back and No.16 Platoon (2/Lieut. H.B.DENNY) was posted by the Commanding Officer on road about X.26 D.5.6. coming under orders of 'B' Company.

3.0 p.m. The Battalion was now disposed as shown on map (Appendix 2), on a frontage of 2,100 yards. No touch had been gained on either flank. Sole available artillery support 2 Anti Aircraft guns. The machine Guns of 'A' and 'C' Companies, 33r .Bn.Machine Gun Corps, were disposed in depth in and behind the Battalion's Front, and throughout the operations rendered very valuable services. The supply of S.A.A. personally arranged by Lieut.Colonel G.S. HUTCHISON, M.C., commanding, was also of very great assistance to the Battalion. Battalion Headquarters established at Farm X.20 b 15.90.

4.0 p.m. One Company 5th.Scottish Rifles, ordered by Brigade to hold position astride METEREN - BAILLEUL Road and to get connection with Battalion's left at cross roads at X 22 c 5 0 since no touch had yet been obtained with troops on right. No. 4 Platoon (2/Lieut. G.F.ASHPITEL) was ordered to take up a position covering bridge at X 20 c, in order to give additional protection to right flank till secured. No.3 Platoon (2/Lt.L.O.PARKES,MC) was ordered up to X 27 b 2 9 to come under orders of O.C.'C' Company as support.

-3-

<u>5.0 p.m.</u> 'B' Company reported enemy digging about 400 yards from their front and apparently being reinforced. Capt. ALLAN went forward to reconnoitre and was wounded, a bullet breaking his thigh. LIEUT. I.T.P.HUGHES assumed command of 'B' Company.

<u>5.32 p.m.</u> One Company 1st.Cameronians was ordered by Brigade to fill gap which existed between Battalion's right and next formed body on right whose identy and position was not definitely known.

'C' Company reported:- "About one Company of enemy advancing on my right". "Am killing them". A party of about 50 stragglers has been collected and put under command of Capt. BETHSON, 8th.Duke of Wellington's on Company's left. No touch yet with 5th.S.R's on left".

Enemy attacked in waves several times but was stopped without difficulty and suffered heavy casualties.

<u>..30 p.m.</u> Brigade ordered 22nd.Corps Reinforcement Camp Details to occupy line. Cross roads, X 22 c 5 0, to STEAM MILL, Z 24 c 11, and covering switch east of METEREN, held by the 5th.S.R's. Touch with the former units was never properly established throughout the operations, only one officer and no other ranks being met. Touch with the 5th.S.R's in switch was gained about this hour.

<u>8 p.m.</u> O.C. 1st.Cameronians assumed command of front from Battalion's right to NORD-HELF X 25, and touch with their left company which was holding a front of about 1000 yards was established at about this hour. A small party of the 9th.Corps Cyclists were present at junction of two units. Although this unit had been ordered to occupy MERRIS and get touch with formation next on right, no confirmation was ever received that this was done. No information or report of any kind was received by O.C. from this unit throughout the operations.

<u>9.0 p.m.</u> Enemy reported all along the front digging in in small posts. Certain localities in front line were shelled by field guns and light T.M's between 7 and 9 P.M. from direction of OUTTERSTEENE and MERRIS both of which places were held by enemy in considerable strength during the night.

<u>10.0 p.m.</u> Two enemy patrols under cover of a fairly heavy bombardment tried to break front of 'B' Company at X 27 d 2 3, both were driven off, identification was obtained from a dead German.

<u>11.0 p.m.</u> Patrol sent out along the whole of the Battalion's front encountered parties of enemy digging in on an average 400 yards from our front. Much enemy activity reported in OUTTERSTEENE. Left flank of Battalion was still more or less in the air owing to non-arrival in position of 22nd.Corps Reinforcements; though this unit was reported by Brigade to be in position at 11.30 p.m. Touch with 'D' Company 5th.Scottish Rifles still maintained.
Shortly before midnight C.S.M. H.ELDERKIN, DCM,MM, was killed while going round the posts held by 'C' Company.

<u>13th.APRIL 1918.</u>
<u>12.35 a.m.</u>   Extract of Q.469 sent to Brigade - "The holding of the front is made precarious owing to the enemy being in occupation of OUTTERSTEENE, from which most of the line is enfiladed AAA I would suggest that, as soon as troops become available, every effort should be made to secure this place and MERRIS AAA I do not consider that I have enough reserve to do this without support as it would greatly lengthen front AAA I consider this of the highest

importance."

<u>4.5 a.m.</u> Situation quiet except for minor patrol encounters.

<u>5.15 a.m.</u> C Company reported to be in touch with post of 5th.S.R's at X 22 c 8 4, but "no sign of 22nd. Corps Reinforcement Company so far".
Enemy using <u>our 18 pounders fairly</u> freely against centre company.

<u>5.30 a.m.</u> Morning very misty. 'D' Company was attacked by two lines of enemy in extended order, strength not definitely ascertained. Attack was driven off by rifle and L.G. fire. Following on this attack, enemy under cover of very considerable artillery and machine gun fire made continual attempts to penetrate the line, but were continually held up. Heavy casualties were inflicted on them during these attempts 'D' Company alone claiming 100 killed and wounded on their front. 'C' Company also inflicted heavy casualties on enemy who tried to cross open ground N.E. of HILL. The mist made observation difficult. The attacking parties on withdrawing apparently moved across the front from our right to left.

<u>6.10 a.m.</u> 'C' Company reported enemy massing on their left and that they had occupied house at X 28 b 20 99. Some of these enemy seem to have broken through 22nd. Corps Reinforcements but as touch with this unit was now re-established, the situation on Battalion's left remained obscure. It is thought that this party suffered too heavily from 'C' Company's fire to make any effective attack. 18th.Middlesex were ordered to counter attack to restore line of 22nd. Corps Reinforcement Company, this attack did not materialise.

<u>7 a.m.</u> One Company 1st.Cameronians was sent to Batt. H.Q. and came under orders of the C.O., and was taken into Battalion Reserve.

<u>8.45 a.m.</u> A Heavy attack developed from the direction of OUTTERSTEENE, strong bodies moving down valley of METEREN BECQUE under cover of heavy artillery and M... fire. Three posts held by "B" Company facing south between X 27 c 41 and 5 0 were overwhelmed. The occupants under 2/Lieut. T.CROMPTON were reported missing, (at time of writing no reports are available as to how these men fared) This necessitated the withdrawal of the remaining posts of 'B' Company. The enemy pressed on down road towards BELLE CROIX FARM in rear of D Company's posts, which necessitated in turn the withdrawal of the posts S.E. of enclosures round BELLE CROIX FARM. This was skilfully carried out. Enemy shortly afterwards occupied farm, two very gallant counter attacks were led against the farm by Lieut. J.A.DICKINSON and 2/Lt. J.H.COREY. These were unfortunately not successful in restoring the situation owing to lack of weight.
During this attack further attacks were also made under cover of heavy artillery preparation on 'C' Company but all were beaten off with heavy loss and the Company's line of posts remained intact. No.16 Platoon also held on to its position on Battalion's right.

<u>9.30 a.m.</u> Message received from 'B' Company that the withdrawal had been "carried out in a quiet and orderly manner". The line now held is shown on map.
In order to restore the situation in the centre of the Battalion, remaining two platoons of 'A' Company were sent forward in support of 'B' Company. These prolonged this Company's line to connect with No.16 Platoon's posts about X 26 d 5 7.

<u>10.30 a.m.</u> One Company of the 18th.Bn.Middlesex Regt., was placed under orders of C.O., and came into Battalion Reserve.

- 5 -

11.0 a.m. Line now held by Battalion was as shown on map (Appendix 3) Owing to withdrawal of 'D' Company on their right, C Company was compelled to withdraw to line of road X 27 d 0 8 to X 22 c 5 0 this was done without interference from enemy owing to heavy casualties already inflicted on them. No touch had been obtained with troops holding main front line on left. No artillery or T.M. support of any kind had yet been obtained.

11.30 a.m. Line now held by Battalion being precarious, C.O. went to Brigade H.Q. After conference with Brigade Commander and O.C. 33rd.Bn. M.G.C. it was decided to withdraw to general line X 26 b 35 to cross roads X 22 c 5 0.

12 noon. One Company 2nd. NEW ZEALAND ENTRENCHING BATTALION put under command of C.O. and dug in west of Battn.H.Q.
Orders for withdrawal to new line issued, to begin at 1.0 p.m.

1.0 p.m. Withdrawal begun, under cover of fire of M.G.Corps and local covering fire.
C.O. going to right flank to supervise withdrawal found situation endangered by enemy attack developing against left of 1st. Cameronians. 2/Lieut. HUGHES and 2/Lieut. DENNY had both been wounded just previously, and 2/Lieut. H.G.SWEET was in command of a mixed party of 'A' and 'B' Companies, and details of 11th. East Yorkshire Regt., which had been collected in this vicinity. The withdrawal to new line connecting with posts already established by No.4 Platoon (2/Lt.G.F.ASHPITEL) was carried out with some difficulty owing to heavy M.G. fire from right front and shrapnel from field guns on road in X 20 c to X 20 d. Posts were finally established as shown on map, App.4. A gap of about 200 yards existing between right of 'D' Company and left of party under 2/Lt. SWEET was covered by a machine gun
Touch with the 1st.Cameronians was very difficult to maintain at this time owing to small force available to man their front.

4 p.m. Remainder of withdrawal completed and touch along Battalion's front established.
Captain H.J.CARPENTER, Commanding 'A' Company was sent forward to control situation on Battalion's right and assumed command of all units to the right of 'D' Company. He was unfortunately wounded soon after taking over command.

4.30 p.m. Enemy under cover of fairly heavy shelling, by our 18 pounders, attacked posts held by 2/Lt. SWEET'S party and posts along hedge X 26 b 3 7 - 9 9 were driven back to a line about 250 yards further back. Farm at X 20 d 1 1 and posts S.W. of it were still held. During this retirement considerable execution was done by a Lewis Gun of No.4 Platoon at X 20 c 8 5.
This withdrawal rendered the dispositions of right of 'D' Company unsuitable and flank was refused on to line of hedge X 21 c 2 1 facing S.W. Guns of 33rd.Bn.M.G.Corps were simultaneously withdrawn entirely from the front line system.
'C' Company, a considerable gap had developed between 'C' and 'D' Companies. No.1 Platoon (2/Lt.C.W.ELLIOTT) was sent up to fill it and came under orders of 'C' Company. Enemy in considerable force was soon moving up from S.E. and they finally established a Machine Gun post at X 22 d 9 2. Any attempt to push on in force was frustrated by fire of our machine guns.
During the afternoon there was very considerable enemy movement all along the front. Parties with machine guns pushing forward with great skill and making full use of ground. Enemy shelling was beginning to be heavy. Several reports of enemy cavalry being in action. These lack any confirmation, though several mounted orderlies were seen.

O.C. 19th.T.M.B. reported with 2 mortars. The position in centre of Battalion was suggested to him; but this he reported untenable owing to machine gun fire. He did not subsequently come into action on Battalion front.

7.30 p.m. Position of centre of Battalion was found very unsatisfactory owing to enclosed country and enemy machine guns on high ground about X 22 d 9 1 and X 25 a 1.5 enfilading the whole of the Battalion's front. It was therefore decided to withdraw centre and left of Battalion, and two platoons 1st.Cameronians and two platoons of 2nd.New Zealand Entrenching Battn. was sent forward to right and left of Battalion's front respectively to strenghten line.
Fresh dispositions as shown on map (App.5) were occupied and dug in by 9 p.m. This operation being carried without difficulty. The withdrawal was effectively covered by machine guns. A supply of tools and wire provided 33rd.Bn.M.G.C. was sent forward, also some rifle grenades.

9 p.m. An artillery liaison officer from a Brigade in action S.E. of METRE reported at Bn.H.Q. and got situation.

9 p.m. to 12 midnight. Situation generally quiet.

14th.APRIL-1918.
12 m.n. to 4.30 a.m. Generally quiet, but patrols reported much enemy activity along the whole front.

6 a.m. Enemy began to mass opposite left centre of Battalion, moving down all roads in strength and deploying. Many excellent targets for machine gun and rifle fire. Posts at X 21 central and X 21 c 8 5 were heavily shelled and trench mortared. Occupants were forced to evacuate them but were shot down almost to a man by enemy machine guns enfilading roads X 22 a 1 0 to X 21 c 5 5. Enemy at once poured down road X 21 c 6 0 - X 21 c 4 5 in strength, and turned left of 'D' Company and right of 'C' Company. Four posts held by 'C' Company in the neighbourhood of farm X 21 c 9 8 were overwhelmed and those withdrawing from them suffered heavily from enfilade machine gun fire already mentioned. Remaining posts held by 'C' Company held throughout the day, and by their fire prevented any further enemy movements in this direction. The situation of right and centre was now extremely critical. (a telephone wire had been run out to H.Q. of 'D' Company and C.O. was kept exactly informed of situation by Capt. H.B.AVERY, who had a very narrow escape of being captured while still talking on this telephone.)
'D' Company had become almost surrounded on its left, but Capt. AVERY with 2/Lieut.CORRY and 25 men fought their way back to trench held by 2 platoons 18th.Middlesex astride road at X 20 b 6 2 which was reached about 8.50 a.m. This party effectively covered its own retreat with fire. Shortly afterwards this party was withdrawn to trenches at X 20 b 8 5.

8.15 a.m. Enemy began to mass opposite right of the Battalion and at about 8.45 a.m. an attack developed but was stopped by rifle and machine gun fire. Many dead were afterwards reported lying out as a result of this attack.

10.30 a.m. The party holding Battalion's right under 2/Lt.SWEET was again attacked, this time in force and with considerable artillery support. The left of these posts having been left more or less in the air by the withdrawal of 'D' Coy. and both 2/Lt.SWEET and 2/Lt. GARDEN, 1st.Cameronians, having become casualties, the most advanced of these posts had to withdraw, falling back through posts of No.4 Platoon.

The latter now, as at all other periods of the operations, held their ground. The mixed parties that had withdrawn from above mentioned posts, were re-organised and put into line of posts on Battalion's right behind No.4 Platoon. Some trenches had previously been prepared here by a Field Coy. R.E.

<u>11 a.m.</u> Enemy had been quick to follow up these withdrawals and had occupied the buildings at X 20 d 1 1, X 20 d 4 7, X 20 d 5 5 and X 21 c 9 9. Machine guns were brought in these houses and several light T.M's came into action in the enclosures round them. Enemy infantry gradually began to accumulate along road X 20 d 5 5, X 21 c 5 1, crawling forward in 2's and 3's. They dug in on this line. Infantry and machine guns held enclosures round farm X 21 c 9 9 and X 21 b 8 0. These carried on a lively fight with our posts further North but made no effort to advance across the open.

<u>12.15 p.m.</u> Two platoons 18th.Bn.Middlesex Rgt. holding trenches astride road X 20 b 2 3 - 8 3, having fired off most of their ammunition at small targets, and having come under M.G. fire from left front, withdrew without warning and for no adequate reason. They suffered several casualties in doing so. Orders were issued for this trench line to be occupied at nightfall by the platoons which had left it. This was done.
The line held at this state, and which was, with some slight modifications, taken over by the relieving battalion, is shown on map (App.6).
Through this morning's fighting touch was continuously maintained with the first Cameronians on right and 5th. S.R's on left.
Liaison with our artillery was established at about this hour for the first time. It was found impossible however, to make effective use of the 18 pdrs. and 4.5's batteries placed at our disposal, as no reconnaissance was done. Communications to batteries was very inadequate and it was found impossible to get artillery fire on any of the targets considered most important by the C.O. A considerable amount of shrapnel was however, fired on neighbourhood of MILL and this had the effect of quietening a few heavy M.G's and doubtless harassed enemy reserves. Co-operation between Boche infantry and gunners extraordinarily good, as was also that between parties working forward in enclosed country with machine guns and batteries of field guns co-operating by means of light signals.

<u>2.30 p.m.</u> Remainder of day passed quietly. Much enemy movement was continually observed opposite whole of Battalion's front. The roof of the farm X 20 b 15 90 which was Battn.H.Q. throughout the operations was an extraordinarily useful O.P.
All targets which presented themselves were dealt with by rifle and L.G. fire. The lack of close artillery support and trench mortars was much felt at this period. Many admirable targets presented themselves, such as machine gun in farms, which could have been easily and effectively dealt with by light or medium T.M's. Enemy artillery and T.M. activity increased considerably during the day, but did not cause many casualties.

<u>4.30 p.m.</u> Capt. WARBURTON, commanding 4th.Bn.King's Regiment, arrived to make arrangements for the relief on night 14-15th.

<u>7.p.m.</u> One platoon 18th.Middlesex was detached as support to 2/Lieut. ASHPITEL to ensure touch being maintained with the 1st.Cameronians, during relief of Battalion, and one platoon 2nd.New Zealand Entrenching Battn. was put into line on the right of 'C' Company to fill a gap that had lasted during day, but which it had been impossible to fill in daylight.
The line held by Battn. and attached troops at time of relief is shown on map 6.

-8-

8.15 p.m. In order to facilitate relief, of Battn.H.Q. moved back to farm at X 15 a 1 0.

9.30 p.m. Platoons of 4th.King's Regt. began to arrive at Battn. H.Qrs.

15th.APRIL 1918.
3.45 a.m. Relief completed without incident. Attached Companies of 1st.Cameronians, 18th.Middlesex, and 2nd.New Zealand Entrenching Battalion returned to their units.
The Battalion was concentrated in NOOTE BOOM Area P 26 d, and billeted in farm. A party of four officers and 87 O.R's of 31st. Division, which had fought alongside the Battalion throughout the operations were relieved, and came out with the Battalion.

DESCRIPTION of COUNTRY. The country over which these operations were carried out is well represented on the 1:20000 map. An agricultural district, entirely under cultivation except the hedge enclosures, shown on map, which are entirely pasture. These pastures are in almost every case enclosed by thick hedges, seldom less than 7 feet high, often lined with high trees, especially on high ground on METEREN - OUTTERSTEENE Ridge.
At the time of operations there was no leaf on the trees or hedges. The ground was all firm and dry.
METEREN BECQUE is a slow running stream about 8 feet wide with firm bottom and banks about 3 - 4 feet high. Fordable everywhere and no great obstacle to infantry.

CASUALTIES.
The following casualties occurred during the operations:-

OFFICERS.	12th. Wounded.	Capt. A.M. ALLAN, Edde W. GREEN. (Both have since died of wounds) 2/Lieut. W.J.C.MORGAN (whilst employed at Brigade H.Q.)
	13th. Killed.	Lieut. J.A.DICKENSON.
	Wounded.	Capt. H.J.CARPENTER, Lieut.I.T.P.HUGHES, 2/Lt. H.B.DENNY.
	Missing.	2/Lt. T.CROMPTON.
	14th. Killed.	2/Lt. C.W.ELLIOTT.
	Wounded.	2/Lts.F.RUSSEN, L.C.PARKES, MC, R.J.BROOKS, H.J.SWEET.

TOTAL OFFICERS - Killed 2.
Wounded 10.
Missing 1. = 13.

OTHER RANKS. Killed 36
Wounded 161.
Missing 160
= 357.

APPENDIX.I

TO: The Chiefs

Sender's Number: NIL
Day of Month: 12

It is reported that the 3rd Division is retiring northward towards METEREN.

2. Move your Battalion at once to take up position covering METEREN in Squares X 20 c, 21 c, 21 d, 22 c, 22 d.
Particular attention should be paid to Right Flank.

3. Send patrols well forward. Position must be held at all costs.
Reference - Sheet 27.

Sgd H Forster BGC
Act. X.6
S.M. 19 Sept 1914

True Copy
R.M. Lee Capt.

SECRET.   BATTALION ORDER NO:79   Copy No: 8
by Lt: Col: M.KEMP-WELCH D.S.O.,M.C.
Comdg: Bn: "THE QUEEN'S" Regiment.
5th April 1918.

Reference Map LENS 1/100,000.

The Battalion will assemble ready to move off in the following order at 11.50 a.m.

"D"   "C"   Drums   "A"   "B"   Transport

Head of Column at "D"Coys most E. billet facing E.
Dress F.S.M.O. Jerkins will be worn. Steel helmets on packs. S.B.R's resting on Packs.

Dinners will be at 11.0am.
Blankets Kits etc to be sent for loading at once.

C.Q.M.Sgts 1 N.C.O and 1 Orderly H.Q. under 2/Lieut: P.J.JAKES will meet Staff Captain at Cross Roads W. of E. in ETRUN at 3.0 pm.

Distances to be maintained during the march, between Coys 100 yards, Rear Coy and Transport 200 yds
Every 5 vehicles in Transport 25 yards.

Destination Camp "Y" N. of DUISANS.   Route via AVESNES le Comte - HARBARCQ.

L.G.Limbers will be with Coys.

Captain & Adjutant.
Battn: "THE QUEEN'S" Regiment.

Copies issued as under -
No:1   O.C. No:1 Coy
  2   O.C. No:2 Coy
  3   O.C. No:3 Coy
  4   O.C. No:4 Coy
  5.   Adjt:
  6.   File.
  7.   War Diary.
  8.   War Diary.

SECRET   Battalion Orders   No 80
                                by
                    Lt-Col. M. Kemp-Welch, D.S.O., M.C.
                    Comdg. Bn "The Queen's" Regt.   Saturday, 6th April 1918

Detail for tomorrow
Subaltern of the Day   Lieut. H. MALLETT

1. Returns   Platoon Commanders will ascertain from their men's Pay Books:- 1. Number of men inoculated within last 12 months (2) Number inoculated more than 12 months ago, but within 24 months (3) Number never inoculated or inoculated more than 24 months ago. Returns to be rendered to Orderly Room by 12 noon 7.4.18.

2. Reversion   205837 L/Cpl. A. Welby, "C" Coy. reverts to Private at own request from this date.
3. Sick   Number reporting sick to day:- "A" Coy. 7; "B" Coy. 7; "D" Coy. 1.

4. Inter-Coy   8797 Sgt. H. Bennett. Transferred from "D" to "B" Coy with effect from 7th inst.
   Transfer.

5. Move.   Ref: Map: LENS, 1/100,000   The Battalion will march to BEAUFORT tomorrow 7th inst via HABARCQ and AVESNES le COMTE. Coys etc will parade ready to move off in the following order at 8.57 AM.
                "B" Drums "A" "C" "D" Lt. H.E.L. DYKE's party, Transport.
                "D" Coy will detail an officer + NCO to take charge of stragglers.
                Dress. Z.S.M.O. Jerkins will be worn, Steel Helmets on packs
                S.B.R. resting on packs.
                Reveille will be at 5.30am. Blankets rolled in bundles of tens packed and labelled ready for loading by 6.45am. Breakfasts will be at 6.30
                Valises + Mess Baskets at B.Q.Stores by 6.45am

6. Billeting   1 NCO per Coy & A'COS, 1 Orderly will parade with Bicycles under
   Party.   Lieut. J.E. Shipton at O. Room at 8.0am and will move as a party.
                Coys will occupy same billets as previously occupied by them.

7. Stores.   All Billet Stores are to be handed back at the same hut from which they were drawn at 6.45am. Receipts to be taken.

8. March   The following distances will be maintained during the march.
   Discipline   Between Coys 100x, Rear Coy & Transport 500x. Between every 6 vehicles 25x. Between Units 500x.

9. -   Attention is drawn to Bde March Discipline Orders.

10. Sanitation O'Cs Coys will ensure huts & ground in vicinity are left clean and sanitary. Lieut. J.E. Shipton will hand over Camp.

11. Details.   Details from BRANDROCK will rejoin in new area.

12. L Guns.   Instructions re Extra Lewis Gun for Anti Aircraft purposes issued to Coys are issued herewith.

13. L.G.Limbers L.G. Limbers will be with Coys.

Copies issued to:
1. CO   2. OC. No 1.   (Sgd) R.H. Nevins Capt & Adjt.
3. OC No.2   4. OC. No 3.   The Queen's Reg.
5. OC. No 4   6. 20
7. QM.   8. Lt. Col. H.E.L. DYKE.
9. RSM   10. Adjt.
11. File   12 & 13. War Diary
14. Spare

                    Certified true copy

                    R.H. Nevins
                    p/p Capt & Adjt
                         The Queen's Regt.

Battalion Orders No 81
by Lt Col. M KEMP-WELCH, DSO. MC
Comdg "The Queen's"
14th April 1918.

1. The Bn will, unless situation materially alters, be relieved by 4th Kings Regt. at any time after 8 pm tonight.

2. Patrols to cover the relief will be put out at least 200x in front from dark and will not be withdrawn until relief is complete.

3. Relief will be carried out by posts and not by units and area Comdrs will ensure that all posts now under his charge are handed over prior to reporting relief complete.

4. On completion of Relief Coys &c will move out via cross roads X 15 a 2.2 (Sheet 27) 200x S of the T in METEREN (HAZEBROUCK) Battalion will concentrate in the vicinity of MOOTE BOOM (R 26 d) 400x N of METEREN. The Company of 2/N 2 Int Rn will rejoin their unit at WINDMILL N of METEREN. Coy 18th Middlesex (Pioneers) will rejoin their Bn. Both these Coys will come under the orders of their respective Bn Comdrs. who will provide guides to conduct them to their destination—

Other Details, except those of & Cameronians who will report Bn H.Q under orders of Coy Cmdr, now with the Battn will accompany the Battalion

- OC Coys will ensure by liaison that
units and all concerned on immediate flanks
know that this is a relief and not a withdrawal. This is not to be published to the
troops until the last possible moment to
avoid any possibility of Enemy obtaining
knowledge of the proposed relief.
- All extra Bandoliers now in possession
will be handed over to relieving troops. Where
possible written notes regarding their position
will be handed over by area Commanders.
7. In the event of an attack taking
place during relief troops who are being
relieved and are withdrawing will turn
about and stand fast in the most favourable
position. Relieving troops will push forward to
their positions.
8. Completion of relief will be reported
Bn H.Q. by code message "uobi"

issued. 7 pm
Nos 6.
OC No.1.
" 3
" 4
Coy N.Z. Sig. Sn.

Capt &

Certified true copy

SECRET   COPY No 6

  Battalion Order No 83
   By Lieut. Col. M.Kemp Welch DSO MC
   Comdg 1st Bn The Queens Regt.
       Friday 19th April 1918

1. The battalion will relieve 4th Duke of Wellington's in reserve position from X.11.b. 8.8. E ST JANS CAPEL Rd (X.6 central) tonight 19th/20th. Companies will be disposed as follows:- Right A, Centre B, Left C, in Reserve at Bn HQ D. A+C Coy will hold the line at all costs; B+D will be at disposal of O.C. Front Battalion for counter attack without reference to Brigade.

2. The battalion will move off in the order H.Q. A B C D. First named will pass Starting Point, A Coy HQ at (R.23.D.5.4) at 11 p.m. Usual distances will be maintained.

3. The battalion will march straight along road to R.36.c.2.5 where guides on platoon scale will be met. In the event of hostile shelling on road companies are reminded that there is open ground across which they may move on side W of road.

4. Relief complete will be sent to Battn. H.Q. by code words "Reply herewith"

5. Bn. H.Q. will be at R.36.c.6.0.

6. Companies are reminded of the necessity of all ranks keeping under cover. Movement must be reduced to a minimum.

J.E. Shipton Lt
a/Adjt
1st Bn The Queens

Copies to
No 1 A Coy
No 2 B Coy
No 3 C Coy
No 4 D Coy
No 5 b.O.
No 6 ⎫
No 7 ⎬ War Diary

Certified true Copy
J.E. Shipton Lt
1st Bn The Queens

SECRET   COPY NO 6

Battalion Order No 84.
By Lieut. Col. M Kemp Welch D.S.O. M.C
Comdg 1st Bn The Queen's Regt
                    Saturday 20th April 1918

1. The battalion will be relieved tonight 20/21st by 321st Regt. As the actual position held by the battalion will not be taken over by the incoming unit, companies will wait until they receive code message "YOUR REPLY AWAITED" when they will move off. O.C. B Coy will be responsible that O.C. A Coy is warned of the receipt of this message.

2. The battalion will march by platoons at 200' interval by route shown on accompanying map in order H.Q. D. C. B. A. to Bttn. concentration area at Q.23.D. If darkness holds a Bttn. concentration area will be allotted in vicinity of PIEBROUCK. Orders for this will be issued on line of march.

3. Lieut P.J. JAKES M.M. will direct march. O.C. D Coy will furnish him with any men necessary to picket doubtful turnings.

4. If it becomes too light to continue march under these arrangements O's C Coys will continue the march

by platoons moving independently, making use of all available cover from view, moving across country if necessary. All unit commanders must know point of concentration.

5. All men will carry out the extra 2 bandoliers at present in their possession.

6. L.G. limbers will be met at X roads at R.28.D.95. 2 men per gun team will be detailed to load guns and equipment on limbers. They will follow with the limbers in rear of their Coys.

7. On arrival at Bdn. concentration area, breakfasts will be issued. Clean socks will be issued, socks will be changed and feet rubbed.

8. While battalion is in concentration area all ranks must be kept under the shelter of hedges or other cover from view. Sentries to give warning of the approach of hostile aircraft will be posted.

Copies to:-
No 1 O.C. A
No 2 O.C. B
No 3 O.C. C
No 4 O.C. D   No 6
No 5 Co.   No 7

SECRET

Battalion Order No.　　　　　Copy No: 13
by Lieut-Col. M. KEMP-WELCH. D.S.O. M.C.
Comdg: 1st "The Queens" Regiment
　　　　　　　　　　　　　　Monday 29/4/18.

1. The Battalion will assemble in the order C. D. Drums A. B. on the open ground in Camp, ready to move off at 9.45 am. and march to RACQUINGHEM Area — Distance about 10 miles via X roads P.31.C. — MONTVECROIX, — V.S.C. — STAPLE — V.7.B. — BOLINGHEM — T.28.b. — BELLE CROIX.
Dress. — S.M.O. Steel helmets on packs, Lewis gun teams will be with Coys.

2. The following distances will be maintained on the march between Coys 100x, Battns 300x.

3. Blankets will be stacked near the Baths under the orders of the QM. at 8.30 am. Each bundle is to be labelled as they are being left behind under a guard furnished by another Battn. Officers Valises to be at QM stores by 8.30 am. Mess Kits will be loaded at 9.0 am.

4. Billeting parties, 1 NCO per Coy & 1 HQ. with bicycles to parade under Lieut J. E. SHIPTON at Orderly Room at 8.0 am.

5. O.C. "B" Coy will detail an NCO. (eff) to collect stragglers should there be any.

Copies issued 7.10 AM.　　　(Sgd) R. A. Nevins Capt & Adjt.
1. C.O.　　2. OC. No 1　　　　"The Queens" Regiment
2. OC. No 2　4. OC No 3
5. OC. No 4　6. QM
7. T.O.　　8. Lt. J.E. Shipton
9. Adjt　　10. RSM
11. File　　12 & 13. War Diary
14. Spare

Certified true copy
R. A. Nevins
Capt & Adjt
1st Bn. The Queens Regt.

Appendix

The following Officers, Warrant Officers, N.C.O.'s & men were brought to notice for devoted, distinguished and gallant service during operations.

No.	Rank	Name	
	Lieut(A/Capt)	V.N.B. AVERY	YES
	Lieut	P.T. HUGHES	YES
	2Lt	T.E. LORRY	YES
		H.B. BENNY	YES
		G.F. ASHPITEL	YES
	Capt	R.H. ALLEN	YES
	Maj	P. RUSTEN	YES
	Lieut	B. MALLET	
340	Cpl	W. HARRIS M.M.	YES
9067	C.S.M.	L.J. BROOKER M.M.	YES
7258	Sgt	H. JONES M.M.	YES
205969	Pte	F.R. BIRCH	YES
14707		T. DUNN M.M.	YES
31009	Pte	A. HUDSON	YES
415	Sgt	J. LAYTON	YES
1049-	Pte	H. HECKER	YES
1571		H. YARRIER	YES
240508	Sgt	C.W. SUTTON	YES
21832	Cpl	P. FARMER	YES
8636	A/Sjt	W.L. HOLLIDAY	YES
22504	Pte	C.A. HALL	YES
10175		A. TAYLOR	YES
34022		F.S. GARDNER	YES
3782		E. CRIST	YES
13052		E.A. GIBBS	
1595		SALES	YES
6234	Pte	H. EDWARDS	YES
10158		W. JARMAIN	YES
9533		J. POWELL	YES
200062	L/Cpl	C. KING	YES
22503	L/Cpl	J. FIELD	YES
43782		F. COX	YES
6266		A.W. GOODWIN	YES
24417	Pte	H. COLLMAN	YES
200870		B. CAWDRAY	YES
18404		G.N. LANGLEY	YES
1835		W. STOKES	YES
7802		H. ELSON	YES
9839		C. MILES	YES
		F. SHEP	YES
1965		T. ALLARD	YES
3599	Sgt	J. WELSH	YES
1019	Cpl	V. DAVIS	YES
17205	Cpl	W.J. TAYLOR	YES
204732	Pte	C. ELLIOTT	YES
25240		A.J. READ	YES
21109		F.R. LAWRENCE	YES
15570	Pte	L. OVEN	YES
15390	Cpl	G.J. SHERRIF	NO
202005	Pte	S. BROWN	
25251	L/Cpl	P. PURDEN	
8086	Pte	W. HOOTEN	
12932		G. HUTCHISON	
3277		G.N. SAUNDERS	
20443		H.S. WILLIS	

W. Kemp-Welch
Lieut Col

25/12/18

Army Form W. 3121.

Schedule No. (to be left blank)	Unit	Regtl. No.	Rank and Name	Action for which commended	Recommended by	Honour or Reward	(To be left blank)

Brigade. _____ Division. _____ Corps. _____ Date of Recommendation. _____

W 13097—4158 100,000 11/15 H W V(P 425) Forms/W. 3121/2
16905—88 200,000 1/16

1st R.W.F.

WAR DIARY
INTELLIGENCE SUMMARY.

MAY 1918 1st Bn The Queens Reg't Vol 43 PAGE 1

Army Form C. 2118.

Place	Date	Hour	Summary of Events and Information	Remarks and references to Appendices
RACQUINGHEM	1		Brigade Orders for move to RACQUINGHEM were received. B.O. issued. Move was completed by 3.30 P.M. Reinforcement of 33 O.R. joined the Battalion.	B.O. 97
— " —	2		Training of normal nature. B.O. warning order for move.	
— " —	3		Move to ABEELE Area received. Bde. Order received & B.O. issued. Captain N.B. AVERY assumed duties of Senior major (vice Major H.E. IRENONGER to Hospital). Battalion moved to STEENVOORDE Area. Personnel by Bus, Transport by road. Arrived L 8 c 2.5 (Sheet 27) and bivouacked. 2 Bo/ans Transport joined up at about 5 p.m. Units stand to move at short notice.	B.O. 99 — " —
Sheet 27 L 8 c 2.5	4		Remained under short notice to move. Inspection re kit.	28 1/R.W.F.
"	5		At 2 hours notice. Stood to man Ry. Lorries to move into Battle Zone. Received orders to be prepared to move about 2pm into close support in G 21 (Sheet 28). Battalion at 2.10 p.m. and marched to G 21. Quartered in a Camp.	An. O. 103

WAR DIARY
INTELLIGENCE SUMMARY
(Erase heading not required.)

1st Battn THE QUEEN'S

Army Form C. 2118.
Page 2.

MAY 1918.

Place	Date	Hour	Summary of Events and Information	Remarks and references to Appendices
	5th		Move was complete by 5 p.m. Minimum Reserve and "B" Echelons moved at 5 p.m. to Camp at L.14.c.4.3.	
G.21.b.	6th		Battn remained in close support. Minimum Reserve at Training and General Routine.	
—	7th		Battn remained in close support. Working party of A, B & C Coys worked on reconnecting STUBERTS HK Switch. Minimum Reserve at Training and General Routine. 2nd Lieut M.B. BLAGDEN and 2nd Lieut C. BRAINGER joined from England – Crawlets 3. OR N.Y.D.(second)	
—	8th		Battn remained in close support. Minimum Reserve at Training and General Routine. About 10.30AM arrival messages received from the Brigade Major to "Stand To" as the situation on the 30th Bn (composite) front was very obscure. AM 12.30 the Battalion was ordered to be ready to move at 10 minutes notice. The Momimuim were ordered to occupy the VLAMERTINGHE line from the Inthn Div Boundary to	

WAR DIARY

INTELLIGENCE SUMMARY. 1st Bn. The Queen's Regt.

MAY 1918 — Army Form C. 2118. **PAGE 3**

Place	Date	Hour	Summary of Events and Information	Remarks and references to Appendices
G.21.b.	8.		HALLEBAST X Roads. 5th S. Lothian Rifles to occupy trenches from the line in squares H.31.A. G.36.B. G.30.C & H.25.C. At 3.15 information was received for a counter attack to be delivered before ourselves for a counter attack to be delivered by 1st Camerons & 5th S.R. in conjunction with 17th King's on left & 98th Inf Bde. on left. This Bn. was to move to more into support in trenches occupied by 5th S.R. as above. The Battalion moved at 5.30 pm was in position at 7.15 p.m. Enemy counter-attack shelling very heavy on position held by this battalion. Casualties 2 Killed. 9 wounded - 21 missing. After attack situation became quieter.	
G.30.D.5.8.	9.		At 3.45 pm orders were issued from Bde. for 2 Coys to be sent to occupy line from HALLEBAST CORNER to N2 central. This was done by 3rd Coys being sent. Move was complete at 6.0 a.m. Situation was received from Bde. Orders were issued by Bde. at 11.35 am for the Bn. to relieve full units or portions of units found in line at from the left of the French (32nd Div) at N.9.3.25.30. Thence right to S.R. at N.3.D.85. In any case the Battalion on relief was ordered to take over the existing line as given above & to push forward to establish a line in front of KLEINE VIERSTRAAT CABT. to form a flank along original front line joining on to the right of the 5th S.R. Particular emphasis was	

WAR DIARY

INTELLIGENCE SUMMARY 1st Bn. The Queen's Regt.

MAY 1918 — Army Form C. 2118. PAGE 4.

Place	Date	Hour	Summary of Events and Information	Remarks and references to Appendices
G.30.d.5.8.			laid on obtaining touch with the French. It was considered probable that elements of the Hanoverians might be found in the original line. I view of the obscure situation the B.O. decided to go forward to the F.A.Q. the various units engaged on the portion B front took reliever and to obtain the latest information regarding the situation to make necessary arrangements for the relief. As the result of this reconnaissance it was found that the line was held by the 17th Kings (30th Composite Bde.) with [keen?] right in touch with the French and 1 Coy of 4th Kings (98th I.B.) just of their left with 5th I.R. The O.C. 17th Kings within his judgment pushed forward his line in the direction of KLEINE VIERSTRAAT C of B. establishing it in front in the manner allotted to the battalion after relieving. This attempt was successful — the line was established and touch gained all along it. As the result of this excellent work the task of the battalion was greatly simplified. It was hoped that the enemy was holding a line about 200x in front. 10th & 11th Coy per Col moves and Sky — touch with the situation on the front line in order to facilitate the relief. Bn. Orders for the relief issued 6 p.m. The battalion moves in to relieve at 10.30 p.m. Relief was complete by 3 a.m. In view of the situation it was desired that the left of the French was conforms with front disposition. On relief it was found that the left of the French was about 150x further to the right than stated & consequently the Battalion of the 33rd French Division on the immediate left contraction. The Battalion of the 33rd French Division on the N.S.W. direction from KLEINE VIERSTRAAT right held a line that turned back in a N.S.W. direction from KLEINE VIERSTRAAT	30.103
N.3.d.4.5.				

WAR DIARY
INTELLIGENCE SUMMARY. 1st Bn. The Queen's Regt.

MAY 1918

Army Form C. 2118.
PAGE 5

Place	Date	Hour	Summary of Events and Information	Remarks and references to Appendices
N3.D.4.5	9		CO Bt. They showed no inclination to advance (a bombing attack ordered for night 9/10th May did not take place). It was found impracticable to advance the Bn line to any appreciable extent without their cooperation. Anyhow we moved up have increased the Battalion's front already held in any every small numbers. Lieut W. PARLOUR. A.S.C. joined from England.	
	10.		About 3.30 am the enemy heavily bombarded the Bn Front, the majority of the barrage falling over the front line. Artillery guidance down about 4.45 am and became normal. Bn sent warning order issued for relief of Bn by 7th French Regt. The O.C. 7/4th Regt came to Bn HQ and details of relief were arranged. Bn. orders issued. About 4.0 pm 2 Bosche enemy were observed to come out of parapet opposite our right D.Coy & to walk towards our line until clear of cover. They were then fired on by No. 14 platoon as was one officer and the other having no line of retreat was captured. They were found to be a battn. commander and an "Officer as prisoner" of the 59th Res. Regt. Artillery. It is presumed that they were endeavouring to locate the exact position of our front lines. About 6.45 pm. O.C. coys (C) coy. observed small parties of the enemy in full packs to be crowding up to the enemy line & considered it probable that a relief was in progress. About 8 pm. the enemy put down a heavy barrage just over on front line. O.C.C by thereupon fires the S.O.S. as he thought the movement he had previously seen might perhaps an attack. The barrage put down by our artillery was exceptionally good, and was effectually	B.O.10.H

WAR DIARY
INTELLIGENCE SUMMARY. 1st Bn. Shropshire Regt.

MAY 1918

Army Form C. 2118.
PAGE 6

Place	Date	Hour	Summary of Events and Information	Remarks and references to Appendices
N30.d.5	10		has dispatched any intention held by the enemy as no infantry action ensued. The situation was quiet & normal again at 8.45 p.m. and for the remainder of the night was abnormally quiet. Bn. Orders for the relief issued. Relief was complete by 3.30 a.m -11.	BO 104
G.21.b & DIRTY BUCKET CAMP A.30.central	11.		The Bn. on relief marched to camp at G.21.B.5.6. Bde Orders for move to DIRTY BUCKET CAMP issued. Bn. Orders issued. Bn moved at 12.42 p.m - move was complete by 3.45 p.m. Minimum Reserve Transport moved to L.9 C.3.6.	BO 105
"	12.		The battalion was bathed today. Minimum Reserve joined the Bn. today. Warning to proceed.	
"	13.		General routine Inspection were held. L.G. & R.G. classes started. Ahead of decoration for operations S. of METEREN on 17/14 th April ensued.	kind of medals appended.
	14.		Training & general routine.	

WAR DIARY

Army Form C. 2118.
PAGE 7.

MAY 1918

INTELLIGENCE SUMMARY. 1st Bn. Sullivan's Regt

Place	Date	Hour	Summary of Events and Information	Remarks and references to Appendices
DIRTY BUCKET CAMP (A.30.Central)	15.		Training & general routine. Lieut F.C. CLUBB reinforcement of 99 O.R. joined today.	
	16.		Training & general routine. During the evening 2 E.A. attempted to bring down one of our balloons. One was brought down by A.A. guns & L.G.'s one of the E.A. was forced to land behind our lines.	
	17.		Training & general routine. Bde. Ceremonial Parade held. Bde. Orders for movt to MATOU area issued. Bn. orders for movt. B Coy. Coy. move out to RUBROUCK for 2 days Musketry Training.	B.O. 112
K.12.d	18.		Bn. moved to new area. Whg's were complete by 9.44 AM. Although weather was extremely hot there were no stragglers. The Battalion were accommodated in tents. 'B' Coy. proceeded by bus to RUBROUCK for 3 days Musketry Training.	
	19.		The Battalion paraded for Divisional Service at 9.15 AM. Afts paraded the Bn. marched past Maj.G.O.C. 19th Infe. Bde.	

WAR DIARY

INTELLIGENCE SUMMARY

1st Bn Shulwiats Regt.

MAY 1918 PAGE 8

Army Form C. 2118.

Place	Date	Hour	Summary of Events and Information	Remarks and references to Appendices
K12b	20		The Brigade was inspected by the Army Commander, General Sir Hubert C.O. PLUMER, G.C.B, G.C.M.G, G.C.V.O. The Brigade was formed up in a hollow square at 11.30am his Add. each of the three sides being a battalion in mass formation. Military Medals were presented to men of the battalion for distinguished conduct in the operations S by METEREN on 12th/14th April. After distributing the ribbons Gen. PLUMER delivered a speech in which he congratulated the 33rd Division & the 19th Brigade upon their excellent work at the critical time 12th/16th April. The battalion marched past around BAILLEUL and METEREN. GEN. PLUMER at the conclusion of this speech A sid a sum football intre platoon competition took place in the afternoon	
	21.		Training & general routine.	
	22.		Training & general routine. Heavy bombardment &Ro	

WAR DIARY

INTELLIGENCE SUMMARY. 1st Bn. The Queen's Regt.

MAY 1918 — PAGE 9

Army Form C. 2118.

Place	Date	Hour	Summary of Events and Information	Remarks and references to Appendices
K12b	22		Held in the afternoon. B Company returned from Musketry + as 2 cubs of smoke had occurred were isolated.	
"	23		Bn. Orders for move to BRAMSHOTT area issued. Training general routine. Bn. orders for movements advance party sent. Capt. G.H. WALLIS, Dem. report the Bn. from ENGLAND.	30. 118
G.11.d.4.2.	24		The Bn. paraded at 3.40 AM marched to ERIE CAMP where they were accommodated. Move was completed by 11 AM. Capt. C. GRANGER left Bn. from 11/5 R. Sussex. Lt. W. PARLOUR left Bn. 2/6 R.S. Brow.	
"	25		3 Companies were engaged upon reconnaissance of defence. Training general routine. Inter-relationships formed for R.E.'s. Notification received of the award of the M.M. to 17453 L/Cpl. J. MOVERLEY.	
"	26		3 Companies were engaged upon reconnaissance of defences. Small working parties for R.E's. Thank. W.J.A. CLAUGHTON joins the battalion. Training general routine.	
"	27		Small parties for work under R.E's around camp. Furnished. Training general routine.	

Army Form C. 2118.
PAGE 10

WAR DIARY
INTELLIGENCE SUMMARY.
1st Bn The Queen's Regt.

MAY 1918

Instructions regarding War Diaries and Intelligence Summaries are contained in F. S. Regs., Part II. and the Staff Manual respectively. Title pages will be prepared in manuscript.

Place	Date	Hour	Summary of Events and Information	Remarks and references to Appendices
G.H.Q.2.	28.		Small parties under R.E's furnished about camp. Training & general routine	
"	29.		A Company provided No. M.T. JES REDOUBTS for musketry practice. Training & general routine. 3 Companies now employed on Lines of Defence. 3 O.R. D. Coy were killed by a shell whilst filed on No 7L Platoon's Hut. Honours for Officers & 3 O.R. in April 12/13th operations received.	List attd.
"	30.		3 Coys. furnished for work on Lines B defence. Training & general routine. 1 O.R. wounded	
"	31.		O's C Coys reconnoitred the front lines. Training & general routine	

W Temp Welch. Lieut Col.
Comdg. 1st Bn. The Queen's Regt.

WAR DIARY

INTELLIGENCE SUMMARY. 1st Bn. The Queen's Regt.

JUNE 1918

Place	Date	Hour	Summary of Events and Information	Remarks and references to Appendices
G.11.D.4.2.	1		Three companies were furnished work upon lines of defence. Training & general routine carried out. Prospectus front reconnoitred by O.C. Coys.	
	2		Training & general routine. B.ks orders for relief by 98th I.B. received. Bn. adm. received. A Coy returned from Murkettig at Mt DES RECOLLETS. Depot A.R.K. EDSELL (East Surrey Regt) joined the Bn.	30.128
RAINSFORD CAMP K.12.6.6.4	3		The Bn. moved to RAINSFORD CAMP. Move was completed by 7.50 A.M. The afternoon was devoted to Regtl. Sports. The Coy competition won by A Coy. D Coy. proceeded by march route & rail to ROEBROUCK for Musketry Practice. Notification received from 100th Inf Bde. that Lance Corpl John M.M. & 8871 Sergt. (A/CSM) T.T. SINCLAIR.	
"	4		Training & general routine. Inter Coy Tug-of-War was held in the afternoon & a concert was given in the evening.	
"	5		Training & general routine. An interplatoon six-a-side football competition was held in the afternoon. B.ks orders for move into the relief of 3rd Yorkshires Regt received.	
"	6		Training & general routine. Teams entered in the open event for sports held by the 5th Scottish Rifles were successful in winning both Officers & O.Rks. Tug-of-War. D. Coy rejoined Bn. from ROEBROUCK. Advance parties sent up to take over the lines.	

Army Form C. 2118.

PAGE 2

JUNE 1918

WAR DIARY
or
INTELLIGENCE SUMMARY. 1st Bn. Influenza Regt.

(Erase heading not required.)

Instructions regarding War Diaries and Intelligence Summaries are contained in F. S. Regs., Part II. and the Staff Manual respectively. Title pages will be prepared in manuscript.

Place	Date	Hour	Summary of Events and Information	Remarks and references to Appendices
RAINSFORD CAMP	6.		Notification of award of the M.C. to Capt. & Adj. R.H. NEVINS published in the London Gazette of 6th inst.	
FWD K.12.A.6.4.	7.		Bn. Order for Relief issued. Training carried out in the morning. Bn. moved up to relief which was carried out without incident & was complete by 3.40 A.M. Front line extends from T.26.c.3.6 & T.27.c.2.9. Supports, Rsrvs, boys in posns just E & W of SWAN Chatn. I.19 & C. Batn HQ at BELGIAN CHAU. in H.23.f. Battn B right 16th K.R.R. on left 5th Scottish Rifles. Situation normal. Minimum rounds round 6.27th. 14.A.20.	BO.133.
29/H.23.6	8.		Situation normal. 1. OR. Killed. Minimum Rounds at Training & Games routine.	
—	9.		Pelican Chateau was periodically shelled during day, after dusk a number of gas shells included in the allotment. Situation normal. No casualties. Drunk seen in huts at Minimum Rounds.	
—	10		Situation normal. 1. OR. wounded. 16th K.R.R. on right relieved by Middx during night. Minimum Rounds at Training & Games routine.	

Army Form C. 2118.

WAR DIARY
or
INTELLIGENCE SUMMARY. 1st Bn "The Queen's Regt.
(Erase heading not required.)

JUNE 1918

PAGE 3.

Place	Date	Hour	Summary of Events and Information	Remarks and references to Appendices
28/H.23.b	11		An exceedingly quiet day. No casualties. Minimum Recont at training & general routine. 2/Lts L. WALKER & J.G. HARKER joined Bn. from Sussex Yeomanry in England.	
28/H.15.b. 9.5.	12		Bn. orders to relief by 1st Cameronians issued. Relief commenced to arrive at 10 p.m. relief was complete by 1.10 a.m. On relief Bn. became came into Bde. Support were disposed as follows. H.Q. A & C Coys in 28/H.15.6. & 16.A. in readiness to move into Front line - H.16.A. - H.11.D. Support in H.16.A. and H.10.C. B & D Coys were in positions in H.17.D & H.18.C. respectively. Rest during day - Attaborn (exl B.18 or.) were furnished by B & D Coys front a GHQ.1 line above SWAN CHAU. 15th (Cand. Scots.) on right 13th/14.5. Bn. Support Rifles in left Subsector.	BO.134
— " —	13	2 A.M.	Casualties NIL. Minimum Recont at training & general routine. Order received for Bn. to relieve 5th Scottish Rifles in Right Subsector.	BO.135
28/H.18.D.4.2.			Relieve 5th Bn. Scottish Rifles in Right Subsector. Relief was completed by 1.45 A.M. The Bn. was disposed as follows. H.Q. H.18.d. 4.2. D (Rifle front) I.27.A.11.— I.21.c.9.0. B (Support) I.21.c.9.0. — I.21.b.0.6. C (Reserve Bn) Battle positions from E.B KRUISSTRAAT try Ry in Allies in KRUISSTRAAT.	

WAR DIARY

INTELLIGENCE SUMMARY
1st Bn. The Queen's Regt.

JUNE 1918 — Army Form C. 2118. PAGE 4

Place	Date	Hour	Summary of Events and Information	Remarks and references to Appendices
2/H.18.d.4.2.	13		Two companies (Cameronians). A. Coy. in view of opposition the carried out on night 15/16th remained in H.15.b. Lieut R.O.V. THOMAS joined Bn. from England. Minimum Reward Trains & general routine.	
—	14.		Situation normal. Reinforcements. Warning Order received for Bn. to be relieved on night 15/16th. Casualties 1 O.R. wounded. Minimum Reward Train & general routine.	B.O. 136
—	15.		Night quiet. 1 officer & 6 yrs or and L.G. team of incoming unit came up to position to be occupied by them on relief. B. orders for relief issued. Day rg quiet. No casualties. Relief commenced at 10.30 pm. Minimum Reward Trains & general routine.	
28/H.7.C.7.0	16		Relief Completed 2.5 AM. Enemy M.G. & artillery more active than usual. No Casualties. A party of Americans (3 officers 44 O.R.) came up on 14th allotted to Front line Coops. They remained in on relief. Anyone any keen lot. On relief Bn. to Frederick Div. Reserve Bn. in manchester/position in squares H.7. - 13. + 14 was settled in by 4 AM.	

WAR DIARY
or
INTELLIGENCE SUMMARY. 10th Bn. The Queen's Regt.

Army Form C. 2118.
PAGE 5

JUNE 1918

Place	Date	Hour	Summary of Events and Information	Remarks and references to Appendices
24H.7C.70.	16.		A Quiet day. Battn in vicinity heavily shelled during evening. 1 O.R. wounded. Minimum Reserve handed at 11.15 AM for Divn Service but owing to rain this had to be abandoned.	
—	17.		Intermittent shelling during night. Battn in I.G.12.D. Baths carried out 2 AM - 7 AM. A & C Coys were shelled during day. No casualties. Minimum Reserve at Training & General routine.	
			A & C	
—	18.		Quiet on the whole. M C Coys commence duties in front on GREEN line cutting entrances in parados & wire. Battn in vicinity of L by heavily shelled during day. A & B Offr & 1 NCO pr Bn HQ & Coy were sent to reconn. support posts of night the front. 1 O.R. wounded. Minimum Reserve at Training & General routine. B & D Coys relieve C & A Coys respectively in position in GREEN LINE.	
—	19.		B & D Coys were engaged on work commenced by A & C Coys on	

WAR DIARY
INTELLIGENCE SUMMARY

1st Bn. The Queen's Regt.

JUNE 1918

PAGE 6

Army Form C. 2118.

Place	Date	Hour	Summary of Events and Information	Remarks and references to Appendices
28/H.7.c.7.0.	19		Orders received Battalion to relieve 4th King's Regt in Support Position Right Bde. Minimum Reserve at Training and general Routine	
"	20		2 Officers 50 O.R and Coy under Lieut H.L DYNE found working party in GREEN LINE in H.13. Lieut Col. M KEMP-WELCH D.S.O. M.C. orders to take over Command of the Brigade took over the duties at 2pm. Command of Battalion reverted upon Captain N.B AVERY M.C. Battalion paraded at 6pm and moved forward in relief of 4th Kings in Brigade Support in H.22 and 23 – in touch with the French on Right and the 100th L.F on Left Relief was completed at 12.45 am. Minimum Reserve at training and general routine.	S.n.O. No 141
H.22d	21		An Exceptionally quiet day – no casualties. Minimum Reserve at training and general routine. 69 O.R. from England joined	
"	22		Situation normal – 1 O.R. wounded Minimum Reserve at Training and general routine	

WAR DIARY / INTELLIGENCE SUMMARY

Army Form C. 2118.

1st Batt. "THE QUEEN'S" Regt.   JUNE 1918   Page 7

Place	Date	Hour	Summary of Events and Information	Remarks and references to Appendices
H.23.d.	23rd		Situation normal — 5 O.R. wounded. Working parties from B.C.T.D. Minimum Reserve attended Divine Service at B'klon 10th L.S. Chby	
L.14.a.0.2	"		Normal — no casualties — Working parties from B.C. and D Coys. and evening	
H.23.d.	24th		BELGIAN CHATEAU shelled with heavy flows during morning & Thures situation Minimum Reserve at Training and general routine	
L.14.a.5.2	"		Lieut Col. M KEMP-WELCH, D.S.O., M.C. whilst temporarily in Command of brigade received instructions to hand over to Lt.Col. T.H. HALL C.M.G. D.S.O. 17th Middlesex Regt and reported at H.Q. 41st Division, having been appointed to command the 122nd Infantry Brigade. Lieut Col. Kemp Welch proceeded the day. Captain A.B. ASHBY struck off not at present appointment as C.M Officer. Lieutenant G. STEVENSON to GRANTHAM — M.G. Course — Struck off. Captain E.S. BINGHAM M.C. joined on receiving appt. Instructor to 5th Army S.O.S. School	
H.23.d	25		Warning order received — GERMAN attack on MT des CATS expected which might involve our front. Ground situation normal — BELGIAN CHATEAU and MOAT FARM Areas shelled during the evening. Minimum Reserve at Training and General Routine	

WAR DIARY / INTELLIGENCE SUMMARY

Army Form C. 2118.

Page 8

JUNE 1918

2nd Battn. "THE QUEEN'S" Regt.

Place	Date	Hour	Summary of Events and Information	Remarks and references to Appendices
H.23.d.	26		Situation Normal – Working parties for R.E. and 5 Coys out at night. No casualties. Minimum Reserve at Training and General Routine. Major G.K. OLLIVER M.C. joined and assumed command of the Battalion.	
L.4.a.6.2	27		Ditto – Our Barrage prearranged came down at 3.30a.m – Enemy reply was feeble. Casualties Nil. Minimum Reserve moved to HULL Camp 2/K.3.d.	
H.23.d. K.3.d.	28		Situation Normal – Working Parties for R.E. and 5 Coys out at night. Casualties NIL. Reserve at Training and General Routine. 2/Lt A.E. SAUNDERS joined.	
"	29		Situation Normal – Working parties for R.E. and 5 Coys out at night. Casualties 2 OR wounded. Others received Bn to be relieved by 16 K.R.R. on night before by 2/Lt H.A.H. CHILCOTT and H.B. ROE. Minimum Reserve at Training and General Routine. 2/Lt C.A. WATTS 8th Bn The E. Surrey Regt. posted to 2nd Bn The Queen's and from C.A. WATTS 8th Bn The E. Surrey Regt.	
"	30		Situation Normal – No Casualties. Relief commenced 11.15 hrs Completed 12.00 hrs. Battalion on relief proceeded to positions in BRANDHOEK area on R. at G.11.d.1.1. Br R.O. 142.	

R.W. Mervyn Capt.
Acting for Lieut. Colonel
Commanding 2nd Bn The Queen's Regt.

Army Form C. 2118.

WAR DIARY
INTELLIGENCE SUMMARY.
(Erase heading not required.)

JULY 1918 1st Batt "THE QUEEN'S" Reg

Page 1.

Place	Date	Hour	Summary of Events and Information	Remarks and references to Appendices
G.H.Q 1.2.	1st	—	RESERVE Bully Grenay Sector. Battalion on relief marched to positions in TORANDHOEK Area with Batth H.Q at G.H.Q 1.2. move was completed at 2.30 p.m. Troops rested by day and were given hot baths (with clean change of underclothing) at night. Quiet day. No casualties.	A.M.O. 142
K 8 d.	2nd		Minimum Reserve at Training and Manoeuvre Ruly 1/15 O.R. under Lieut T.E.CORRIE proceed to 2nd Army Rest Camp at AUDRESSELLES. Rifles and one Lewis Gun of Armament and Equipment. Sanitary condition of Company's arms inspected. Captain N. BAVERY, M.C. (Accompanied by Armourer) inspected England & open Senior officers class — struck off. Lieuts S. ROBINSON and F.G. HARTLEY posted to 1st R. E. Surrey Regt - the first supposed the July the latter was at Army Chemistry School 15 Jm wounded on completion — October off. Lewis Gun classes commenced 32 O.R at H.Q and 32 at C.H.R. Minimum Reserve strength over. Lieut H.G.A MARSHARD and Lieut. S.G.W. HUNT joined from England.	
Do	3rd		Working Parties 2 Officers 75 O.R. for C.R.E. — furnished for work under R.E. for Defences Purposes in G 12 d and K 13 d. Minimum Reserve at Training R.C	30 1/RWS

WAR DIARY

JULY 1918

INTELLIGENCE SUMMARY

(Erase heading not required.)

7/7th "The Queen's" Regt

Army Form C. 2118.

Page 2

Place	Date	Hour	Summary of Events and Information	Remarks and references to Appendices
G.11.d.1.2	4th		Working Parties 2 Officers 75 O.R. 1st Coy were furnished for work under R.E. on defensive line in G.12.d and H.13.a. Minimum Reserve at Training &c. During the afternoon Minimum Reserve moved joining "B" Echelon in L.g.c. 2/Lieut H.S. LEWIS joined from England. Bttn relieved Battalion will take over front line from I.21.d.1.1/2 to I.26.a.1.1/2 Railway relieving Right Front Coy of Kings and left front at 1.7pm. Coy of Kings in I.19.b and I.19.d. 2/Lieut A. SLIGHTS 1 Coy of Kings in G.H.Q.1 line in I.13.c and I.19.a. 4 Kings in G.H.Q.2 line in I.13.c and I.19.a. ⟨illegible⟩ 4 Officers & Capt (a/Maj) H.ETREMONGER joined from England. Situation normal – no casualties.	Bn.O. 148.
Front line Pm.H.2 H.24.6-4.8	5th		Relief was carried out without incident and completed at 2am. Situation normal – no Casualties. Minimum Reserve at Training.	
—	6th		Quiet day – At about 11.45pm our Artillery put down a Barrage in connection with minor operation carried out by 9th H.L.I. in Sector on Right of Battalion. Hostile reply fell on our Left front Coy "C": two casualties. 4 Officers 6 O.R. American Army (117th Regt) attached to p 48. Reserve at Training	

Army Form C. 2118.

Page 3.

WAR DIARY
JULY 1918

INTELLIGENCE SUMMARY.
1st Battn "The Queens"

(Erase heading not required.)

Place	Date	Hour	Summary of Events and Information	Remarks and references to Appendices
FRONT LINE Fr. N.8.H.24 to 4.8	7		Quiet day — Minimum Reserve at Training — No casualties.	
"	8		Quiet day — at night a patrol of Regt front by "A" whilst returning own No mans land sustained 2 casualties. 1 O.R. killed 1 O.R. wounded. Instructions received that Battalion to furnish a Company strength 6 officers 213 other ranks which with other contingents is to form a Composite Battalion representing the British Army in France at the Demonstration taking place at Paris on 14th July 1918. Company to leave on 9th. Battalion to be relieved tonight 8th/9th by 5th Bn Scottish Rifles. Relief commenced 9.20pm carried out without incident completed 3.50am	M.O.600 4.
Support Scottish N-B-H.15 to 9.5	9		On relief Battalion moved into Brigade Support Coys disposed as follows "B" H.19 & B.H.18.c "A" and "C" in the vicinity of Bn H.Q. H.15 & 9.5. 2 officers 200 O.R. working parties under R.E. on G.H.Q.1 line and BROWN Line Water occupied by "A" Coy heavily shelled during afternoon Casualties Lcpl H. Lewis Severely	

WAR DIARY   JULY 1918.

INTELLIGENCE SUMMARY 1st Batt "THE QUEEN'S"

Army Form C. 2118.   Page 4

Place	Date	Hour	Summary of Events and Information	Remarks and references to Appendices
Support H.15 c - 9.5	9		Severely Wounded. Minimum Reserve at Training	
"	10		Working Parties furnished – 3 O.R. killed by aerial bit on a "O" Coy furnes. Lieuts: H.L.C. WHITTAKER, NORTH, Lieut W.H. COURTHOPE and 70 O.R. joined Captain H.E. DRESING M.C. R.a.m.C. (S.R.) relieves Captain G.C. GAYNOR M.C. R.a.m.C. (S.R.) as Medical officer i/c Battalion. Minimum Reserve at Training	
"	11		Working Parties furnished. No casualties. No. 640 P.W. CREASEY selected to represent 2nd Army v Belgian Army in Cross Country Run. Minimum Reserve at Training.	
"	12		Working Parties furnished – No Casualties – Minimum Reserve at Training. Captain R.H. PHILPOT M.C. joined and took up the duties of Major on H.Q.rs Minimum Reserve at Training.	
"	13		Working Parties furnished – No Casualties – Minimum Reserve at Training.	

WAR DIARY JULY 1918.

INTELLIGENCE SUMMARY

by Battn. The Queen's

Page 5.

Army Form C. 2118.

Place	Date	Hour	Summary of Events and Information	Remarks and references to Appendices
Support H.15.b.9.5.	14th		Working Parties furnished Casualties Lieut. W.A. NORTH and 2 O.R. wounded. — Minimum Reserve at Training.	
— " —	15th		Quiet day — no casualties — Minimum Reserve at training — Bn. Received Battalion to be relieved by 2nd K.S.L.I. tonight and on relief Moved to CARRIER Camp. (G.11.d.) — Relief carried out — completed 11.20pm	M.O. 005.
Rein. Reserve G.11.d.	16		Working Parties furnished — No Casualties — Minimum Reserve at Training	
— " —	17		— Ditto —	
— " —	18		Quiet Day — no Casualties — Lieut. C. JACKSON left for England to form M.G. Corps — Minimum Reserve at training — Company reported after taking part in demonstration at Paris.	
— " —	19		Working Parties furnished — Aeroplane Photographs shown Bn. by H.Q. carried out no Casualties — M. [signature] — Minimum Reserve at Training.	

Army Form C. 2118.

Page 6

WAR DIARY

INTELLIGENCE SUMMARY

of 1st Bn. R. Fusiliers Regt.

JULY 1918

(Erase heading not required.)

Place	Date	Hour	Summary of Events and Information	Remarks and references to Appendices
Div. Reserve G.11.d.	20		Instructions received Battalion to relieve pt. 2nd Middlesex Regt in Right Sub-sector — Canal Sector tonight — Relief commenced 10.15pm Completed 1-30am. Coys disposed as follows RIGHT FRONT "B" — LEFT FRONT "D" SUPPORT "C" RESERVE "A" Battn H.Q. at H.24.c.7.2. N.R. at Training	A.O. 150
Front Line Bn. H.Q. H.24.c.	21		"D" Coy 111th American Regt were taken over in the line one platoon with each Coy. Support Coy & Bn H.Q. areas were shelled intermittently during day — our Artillery put down too Counter Preparation Shoots which ended lively retaliation on Support Coy & Bn H.Q. area — Casualties 10 O.R. Killed 2 O.R. wounded. Minimum Reserve with Trainings attached. Divine Service 10am.	
— " —	22		Quiet up to 5.30pm when an Area Shoot was put down on Support Coy. Casualties 7 O.R. wounded. Minimum Reserve at Training — Captain E.W. BETHELL joined.	

WAR DIARY JULY 1918

INTELLIGENCE SUMMARY. 1st Bn. The Queen's Regt.

Army Form C. 2118.
Page 7.

Place	Date	Hour	Summary of Events and Information	Remarks and references to Appendices
Front Line Sub.Sect.C.	23		Intermittent shelling 8 O.R. wounded. Minimum Reserve at Trenning.	
"	24		Quiet day. 2 Coy 2/119th American Regt attached for instruction. Casualties 2 O.R. Minimum Reserve at Trenning.	30/5/9
"	25		Quiet day. Coy 1 O.R. wounded. Considerable movement of Enemy during the night who dealt with by Rifle L.G. Grenade T.M. fire. Minimum Reserve at Trenning.	
"	26		Quiet day. Casualties 7 O.R. wounded. Minimum Reserve at Trenning - Battalion relieved by 1st Bn Cameron. Rely-Compl(d) 2.20am Bn relief. Battalion moved into Bugra Support occupying position in H.21, 22 and 23. Bn. H.Q. and A Coy in H.23.d. B Coy WHITE CHATEAU C Coy ANDES Fm D Coy SMYTHE Fm Slight shelling of H.23.d. Working parties furnished. Minimum Reserve at Trenning.	Ro. 152
"	27			

H (A/Capt) T.P. NEWMAN D.C.M. Aliquated Burenery A/G. Cmdg 1st Bn The Queen's Battalion

Army Form C. 2118.

Page 8

WAR DIARY July 1918

INTELLIGENCE SUMMARY of 7th. "The Queen's Regt."

(Erase heading not required.)

Place	Date	Hour	Summary of Events and Information	Remarks and references to Appendices
Support H.23.d	28		Quiet day - Working parties furnished - No casualties - Minimum Reserve at Training and Divine Service	
"	29		Quiet day - Working parties furnished - No casualties - Bde Order in lieu received - Minimum Reserve at Tr'g	
"	30		By orders received Advance parties 16th KRR took over stores during afternoon. Small parties furnished. Relief however effected fairly quickly and was complete at 10.50 p.m. Bn relief the Bn works the Divisional Reserve area A C & D Coys we concentrated in vicinity of the YELLOW LINE B.6.d at LEVER FARM and a Coy HQ at ERIE FARM work this area was complete by 1 AM. Casualties Nil	30 1 33
ERIE FARM	31		Holiday up and training occupied the day	

WAR DIARY

Army Form C. 2118.

JULY 1918

PAGE 9

INTELLIGENCE SUMMARY. 1st Bn. The Queens Rgt.

Place	Date	Hour	Summary of Events and Information	Remarks and references to Appendices
ERIE FARM	31		Baths were allotted to the Bn. and the Prisoner Intakes inspected the Lewis Gun rifles. Major P.C. ESDAILE joined the Bn. as second in command. Casualties nil.	

P.C. Esdaile, Major
Comdg. 1st Bn. The Queens Rgt.

Army Form C. 2118.

WAR DIARY

INTELLIGENCE SUMMARY

19/33 AUGUST 1918

1st Bn. The Queens Regt.

98 46

Place	Date	Hour	Summary of Events and Information	Remarks and references to Appendices
ERIE FARM	1		Working parties of 5 Officers & 250 O.Rks furnished for work on GREEN and YELLOW lines. A party of 3 Officers and 46 O.Rks proceeded to St MALO BAINS for a day by the sea side. Capt. E.W. BETHELL assumed command of B Coy. Training and general routine carried out. Casualties nil. Capt. G.F.A. SHPITEL M.C. proceeded to H.Q. 3/20 American Regt. for attachment. Reserves was changed.	
2H.II.D.0.1	2		Working parties of 5 officers and 250 O.Rks furnished for work on GREEN and YELLOW lines. Training was hampered by the inclement weather. Casualties Nil.	
	3		Day devoted to Company training in view of attack being this Nth Bde. Orders issued re relief of 98th of Bde. Reconnre parties sent up to take over	31 1/PWS

WAR DIARY AUGUST 1918   Army Form C. 2118.

INTELLIGENCE SUMMARY. 1st Bn. The Queen's Regt. PAGE 2

(Erase heading not required.)

Place	Date	Hour	Summary of Events and Information	Remarks and references to Appendices
ERIE FARM 3. 26/4.11.D.0.1.			from 4th Bn The King's Regt.	
	4.		Bn. Orders for relief of 4th King's issued. Bn moves B at 8.0 p.m and relief was completed by 1 a.m. 1st J.K. Corps. 9/10 American Regt. were taken over in the line and in order to prevent occupying of the position a proportionately large Minimum Reserve was to be left out. On relief Coys were disposed as follows:- Right Front "A"; Left Front "C"; Support "D"; Reserve "B". Bn. HQ was at H.24.B.6.9. Reconnaissance detgt OLIVER was detailed as markers at a ceremonial Church parade service held at in commemoration of the 4th Anniversary of the war	30.156.
	5.		Minimum Reserve at "Dorme" & several routine Situation Normal.	
H.24.b.6.9	6.		The enemy attempted a raid & post held by "A" Coy During day severe intermittent but was driven off	

WAR DIARY
INTELLIGENCE SUMMARY. 1st Bn. The Queen's Regt.

AUGUST 1918   PAGE 3

Place	Date	Hour	Summary of Events and Information	Remarks and references to Appendices
H.28.b.9.6.	6.		Shelling of KRUISSTRAAT area. Preparations for special operation made — but this was cancelled and fronts re-occupied. The enemy proved himself very active in patrolling + being anxious to secure an identification. Counter preparation was put down during night on enemy's defences. Casualties 2 OR wounded. Minimum reserve were called upon to furnish a party to proceed to LOVIE CHATEAU + line the Avenue to cheer H.M. the King as he passed along. Lieuts F.C. GWEBB + M. BRAGDEN were i/c parties and 100 OR were selected. Party left Regiment. Train was carried out during morning. Capt. G.F. ASHPITEL MC rejoined.	B.O. 159.
"	7		The Charge over John American Bzyr. was decided upon + other coincident changes. These were carried out without incident. Relief was completed by 1.30 AM. Casualties NIL. Minimum Reserve at Training huts W.A. North.	B.O.16

WAR DIARY AUGUST 1918 Army Form C. 2118.

INTELLIGENCE SUMMARY. 1st Bn "The Queen's" Regt.

Place	Date	Hour	Summary of Events and Information	Remarks and references to Appendices
28H24b 6.9	8		Situation normal. Casualties Nil. Command American Troops paraded to OC 3/120 American Regt at 8 pm. Minimum Reserve at Training.	30.161
	9		Our Artillery carried out a bombardment of VOORTIZEELE and defences during afternoon. Hostile Artillery active infront of left (B) Coy during night. Casualties 3 OR killed. Bde order for relief 9/3/20 = American Regt to relieve 10/11s received. The Queen's + 1st The Cameronians will then take over original positions. B Coy relieve C Coy as relief was complete at 1.25 AM. Minimum Reserve Trained.	30.162
	10		Quiet day. Great activity in the air late afternoon. Troops recupied normal positions on relief	20.163

WAR DIARY

INTELLIGENCE SUMMARY

AUGUST 1918 — "Fullerene" Regt

PAGE 5

Place	Date	Hour	Summary of Events and Information	Remarks and references to Appendices
28/4.21. 5.6.9.	10 (cont'd)		Of 3 coys 2/S.African Regt moved Company at 9.30pm. The consolidating coys were deployed: Right Front S Coy; reserved Left Front – Support A Coy – Reserve C Coy. Relief was complete at 1.30am. Minimum arms at training and funeral services. Bn was detailed to furnish a working at ceremonial parade at HONDEGHEM. Sgt. HURST was detailed.	
"	11		Minimum Reinforcements arriving at 11 am for Divine Service. Quiet during the day. Patrols out during the day did not encounter any of the enemy. No 1 Post was handed over to the 1st Cameronians (Ry'ls Bn). Great aerial activity during the evening. Low flying machines over Bn HQ heavily fired on by AA L.Guns. No casualties.	
"	12		Quiet day. Privates J.A. BROOKES and A. BASSETT joined Bn from England. One of our patrols out	

Army Form C. 2118.

PAGE 6

AUGUST 1918

1st Bn Mullineux Regt

WAR DIARY

INTELLIGENCE SUMMARY
(Erase heading not required.)

Place	Date	Hour	Summary of Events and Information	Remarks and references to Appendices
B.6.9.	28/H.21 12 (cont)		During the night a patrol lying out discovered a large party of the enemy crawling towards them evidently intending to raid one of our posts. On fire being opened the party retired but owing to darkness fire effect could not be observed. No casualties. Minimum Reserve at Training.	
	13		Quiet day. Our aircraft active. Orders received for Bn to be relieved on night 14th/15th by 2 companies 6th HLI and 2 companies Lopo by chats. Advance parties on incoming units arrived. Battalion views issued. Minimum Reserve at Training	BO164
	14		Quiet day. Enemy shelled KRUISSTRAAT during the relief and inflicted casualties on the incoming unit. Relief was complete at 3.0 AM	

WAR DIARY

INTELLIGENCE SUMMARY.

AUGUST 1918
1st Bn. The Queen's Ryl.
PAGE 7
Army Form C. 2118.

Place	Date	Hour	Summary of Events and Information	Remarks and references to Appendices
KNOLLYS Fm	14/15		On relief the Bn. marched to BRANDHOEK area.	
H.T.C.	15		Dispositions Left Front Coy (A) LEVEL Fm. Right Front 16 Coy (C) LEVEL Fm. Support Coys B & D at PEMMICAN Fm and D at KNOLLYS Fm. BnHQ at KNOLLYS Fm. Move was complete at 4.45 AM. During the morning B was employed in clearing up. At 12.30 PM a warning order was received regarding relief of Bn in BRANDHOEK area by 3/119th American Ryt. on night 15/16th. Bde Orders went for relief. B & D to be relieved for relief. Bn. relieved by Kt.K5. over HUSBAND camp in Advance party - Advance party 3/119th American Ryt. arrives 5pm. On relief Bn. proceeds marching to ROOSENDAAL area.	Bo.106 Bo.106
HUSBAND CAMP	16		Move was complete at 2.0 AM. Morning occupied in training. Afternoon Winner Reserve returned.	
H.T.S.24				

WAR DIARY
INTELLIGENCE SUMMARY. 1st Bn. The Queen's Regt.

Army Form C. 2118.
AUGUST 1918
PAGE 8

Place	Date	Hour	Summary of Events and Information	Remarks and references to Appendices
HUSBAND CAMP 31/L.7.D.2.2.	16 (contd)	9 AM	The Bn at 9 AM. The Armourer Sergt was allotted to Companies. Reorganisation of B. under WE 1919 completed.	CAMP APPT
	17		WESTGATE BATHS were allotted to the Bn and all men underwent training was carried out except when actually at the Baths. Bn. order for movement to EPREIECQUES Sub-Area issued.	
	18		The Transport less Cookers HQ limbers & water carts commenced march by road three ams. Advance party moved by lorry to GANSPETTE and thence bicycle to MENTQUE Bn advance party moved by road via MENTQUE.	BO 169
	19		The Bn paraded at 12.30 PM and marched to MENDINGHEM Station where entrainment was carried out. Detained at MATTEN at 7.30pm entrained for (?) and reached K.MENTQUE at 8.10pm — debrakis was reached at 11.25pm	

Army Form C. 2118.

PAGE 9

WAR DIARY
INTELLIGENCE SUMMARY.
AUGUST 1918 1st Bn Mullen's Regt

(Erase heading not required.)

Place	Date	Hour	Summary of Events and Information	Remarks and references to Appendices
MENTQUE	19/8/18		Move was complete and men settled in at 12 midnight. Bn. Orders for move 5 LICQUES men issued.	Bn Orders 30,190
	20		Advance party proceeded to SANGHEN and ALEMBON to prepare for move. Bn moved at 10 A.M. and marched by new road. The Bn arrived at 3.45 pm and troops were accommodated. Bn HQ A+B at SANGHEN and C+D Coys at ALEMBON. Ammn Transport & companies cookers in by 4.30 PM. Move was complete.	
SANGHEN	21		The day was spent in cleaning up and administration.	
"	22		Training and general routine carried out. All officers attended at Demonstration showing firing by	

WAR DIARY

INTELLIGENCE SUMMARY

AUGUST 1918 Army Form C. 2118.
PAGE 10.
1st Bn. The Queen's Regt.

Place	Date	Hour	Summary of Events and Information	Remarks and references to Appendices
SANGHEN	23 (contd)		Brig Genl DUGGAN with administration platoon.	
-	24		Reinforcement of 1 Offr (Sec Lieut A.F. FIELD) and 112 O.R's joined Bn. from Div. Reinforcement Camp. Training and general routine carried out. One half of the Battalion who bathed at N.C.O/U.R.S Baths.	
-	25		Inspection and ceremonial parade. The Battalion paraded at 9.15 A.M. on ground in 22a/N.13 for Divine Service. The parade was attended by Lieut Col Rejoined Bn. Remainder of Bn. bathed at NCO/O.R.S BATHS.	
-	26		Warning orders received from Bde regarding preparation for sudden move 12.30 A.M. Warning orders received that the Division will entrain on 27th inst. Advance parties sent	80/75

WAR DIARY

INTELLIGENCE SUMMARY. 1st Bn. The Queen's Regt.

AUGUST 1918 Army Form C. 2118.

PAGE 11

Place	Date	Hour	Summary of Events and Information	Remarks and references to Appendices
SANGHEN	26 (contd)		forward to LUMBRES area. Bn Orders for move to SENINGHEM were issued at 5.30 pm and move was complete by 11.15 pm. Personnel from 11th Lancs Regt joining Full Cdr.	B.O. 176
SENINGHEM	27		Day spent in resting and cleaning up. Bde Order for move by road to WERGNY area received. Bn. joined 10th Coy was detached at Bde loading party and proceeded to WIZERNES station at 2.30 pm in advance parties provided lorry for the new area.	B.O. 177
	28		Bn proceeded ordered entrainment at WIZERNES Station. After assault of 4th Coy entrainment was proceeded with and train moved off at 5.25 pm. The detraining station (FRÉNENT) was reached at 12 midnight.	
	29		After detraining the Bn had ten minutes of	

WAR DIARY
INTELLIGENCE SUMMARY. 10th Bn Sullivan's Rgt.

Army Form C. 2118.
AUGUST 1918
PAGE 12

Place	Date	Hour	Summary of Events and Information	Remarks and references to Appendices
NERGNY	29 cont'd	1.15 AM	to NERGNY Mov was complete at 4.0 AM. 'C' Company proceeded by the lack from Leaving WIZERNES and reached our area at 5.15 PM. The remainder of the day was spent in cleaning up and inspections.	
(LENS 11. 1/100000)	30		The Battalion paraded at 9.15 AM when all ranks to take part in a Brigade Ceremonial Parade for the distribution of ribbons by the G.O.C. Infamous Major General L.R. Rawnsley PINNEY, K.C.B. The Ribbon were "pinned on" and "boxed up" to S in LE SOUICH the following were the recipients:— Military Cross Capt. & Adj. R.H. NEVINS, Capt. G. FASHPITER 2nd LIEUT. J.E. CORRY Distinguished Conduct Medal 2/LIEUT. I.T. BROOKER M.M. 9238 L/Sgt. H. JONES M.M., 3710 Sgt. L. HARRIS M.M.	

WAR DIARY
INTELLIGENCE SUMMARY AUGUST 1918 Army Form C. 2118.
1st Bn The Queen's Regt PAGE 13

Place	Date	Hour	Summary of Events and Information	Remarks and references to Appendices
NERGNY	30 (contd)		Bar to Military Medal 39791 L/Cpl. C COTTINGHAM M.M. Military Medal 37009 Sergt. A. HUDSON, 1743 Sergt. J MOVERLEY, 3715 Sergt. T. LAYTON, 6125th Cpl W EDWARDS 205064 L/Cpl. G. KNIGHT, 139.24 Pte E. SALT 22322 Pte H. ELSON Meritorious Service Medal 8255 Sergt. A BENSON The remainder of the day was spent in training.	
	31		Training and general routine were carried out	

R. Powse
Lieut Col
Comdg 1st Bn The Queen's Regt.

WAR DIARY
or
INTELLIGENCE SUMMARY.

Army Form C. 2118.

SEPTEMBER 1918

PAGE 1

1st Bn. The Queen's Regt.

9647

33 1/RWS

Place	Date	Hour	Summary of Events and Information	Remarks and references to Appendices
VERGNY (LENS) 1:10000	1		Training and final lecture carried out during morning. All officers and Senior NCO's attended a lecture held at Bn HQ 9.30 if possible on Co-operation between Tanks and Infantry at 6 pm.	
"	2		Training throughout carried out during day. An exercise for the 16 Scouts under Sergt Rose held in Bivouac at 6.30 pm.	
"	3		Bn less "A" Coy on tactical exercise at 8.30 am on the VERGNY - LE SOUICH Rd. as marched back to their lines in the vicinity of Latre nememourn village about 5 p.m. Tactical exercise being carried out. Musketry training carried out during afternoon	

Army Form C. 2118.
PAGE 2

WAR DIARY
INTELLIGENCE SUMMARY

SEPTEMBER 1918 1st Bn. "Queens" Regt.

(Erase heading not required.)

Place	Date	Hour	Summary of Events and Information	Remarks and references to Appendices
MERCATEL (LENS 11) (1:100,000)	4		Baths to accommodate about 75% of the Battalion were allotted to Bn. at LUCHEUX. Baths in the interval. Companies were employed at training and musketry & rifle grenade practice to be carried out. All officers attended a lecture at Brigade H.Q. at SOUICH at 5 p.m. by Major BOYD-ROCHFORT, DSO MC on "Tanks".	
	5		Lieut ROE THOMAS rejoined the Bn from hospital. The C.O, Adjutant and 9 officers proceeded from KWAYRANS to see a tank demonstration. Training general. Routine was carried out.	
	6		A Brigade Tactical exercise was held on ground S of RE VILLERS. The Battalion furnished 7m and marched to recently positions in valley N.E GROVES	

WAR DIARY
INTELLIGENCE SUMMARY

SEPTEMBER 1918
1st Bn Thull men's Regt.

Place	Date	Hour	Summary of Events and Information	Remarks and references to Appendices
VERGNY (LENS II 1:100,000)	6 (cont)		Attack on Bois de Rebymont continued & eventually accomplished to lack by dawn, when BREVILLERS and Le SOUICH were the objective which were reached about 1 pm, when troops were ordered to close and march home.	
	7th		Training and General Routine	
	8th		Ditto — Weather being inclement outdoor duties were omitted	
	9		Training and General Routine	
	10th		Ditto	
	11th		Ditto	
	12		Ditto	

WAR DIARY / INTELLIGENCE SUMMARY

Army Form C. 2118.
SEPTEMBER 1918
1/5 Bath. THE QUEEN'S Regt
Page 4

Place	Date	Hour	Summary of Events and Information	Remarks and references to Appendices
IVERGNY	13		Training and General Routine – S.B.R's &c. were tested by all ranks. Morning through Gas Chamber. All Officers and N.C.O's attended lectures by Divisional Commander at 5th N.R. 5.30pm Subjects dealt with were "The Situation". "The role the Division was likely to fulfill in the near future." – "Eyres" & "Battle during the Battle of Ypres." Lieut W.J.C. MORGAN rejoined from wounded re: from wounds rcd 13/3.	
"	14		Orders received Battalion to be prepared to move on night 14/15 "Warn" by road or Rail. Transport marched at 6pm. Move by Bus carried out vide WARNING ORDER – Bn Entrained by 9.30pm	W/5 Oppr
"	15		Column started 10.30pm arrived MANAN COURT at 7.30am detrained and went into Bivouac at X 9 central Sheet 57 C. Warning orders received Bn to relieve 110" L.F. in Front Line tonight. Transport halted at HEDAUVILLE – marched again at 7pm. 6 L.G. TRANSLOY. Battalion paraded at 7.45pm and took over front line (Sheet 57 C.S.E. W 23.a.8.0 Gr.O.163 6 W.18.a.7.3) from 6th Bn Leicestershire Regt. Coys were disposed A Right C Centre D Left	

WAR DIARY

INTELLIGENCE SUMMARY of Batt. The Queen's Regt

Army Form C. 2118.

SEPTEMBER 1918

Page 5.

Place	Date	Hour	Summary of Events and Information	Remarks and references to Appendices
Front Line	15th Contd.		B Support W.23 Central. Bn. H.Q. at W.21 c.1.1. Relief was completed at 1.30am. Minimum Reserve under Major G.K. OLIVER M.C. paraded at 7am. 15 marched to	
	16th		BEAULEN COURT. Transport arrived MANANCOURT. Weather much improved – night 15/16th Situation normal – Great activity in the air during the night – a great deal of hostile bombing. Casualties Nil.	
	17th		Quiet day – Orders received Battalion would be relieved night 16/17 by Sub. R.D. Bde. 62nd Inf. Bde. Relief Commenced 9pm from Battn. H.Q. Reported complete 5am though it was accompanied by a Storm. A violent Rainstorm broke at about 2am and rain fell in torrents – the night was no slack. Left Front Coy 'D' occupied no less than 3 hours making the journey from Support Coy area to Bn. H.Q. having been forced to march in a compass bearing. On relief Bn. marched to billets at MANANCOURT now completed at 9.20am. Troops at rest remainder of day. Bn. received Battalion to be in readiness to move forward early Bn. 18 Inst.	

WAR DIARY

INTELLIGENCE SUMMARY

1st Batt "THE QUEENS" Regt

SEPTEMBER 1918   Army. Form C. 2118.

Page 6.

Place	Date	Hour	Summary of Events and Information	Remarks and references to Appendices
MANANCOURT	18.		Battalion moved to assembly position in W.17.d. Move completed about 7am. Remained on this ground for the day. Operations in progress. Enemy pressing troops during day from 2nd Divn Front.	ApD.165
"	19		Battalion moved forward to low ground in W.26.a across country in Artillery formation – move completed 7.35am. Warning order South to relieve 6th in Keicots 110th L.B. tonight. Moved leaving Kalari 7.30pm. Relief completed at Midnight. Quiet except no Casualties. Maj G.K. Othen M.C. joined Bn. Minimum Keebo.	ApO.166. Bro 167
Front line X.19.c3.2	20		Warning order received that we would attack on 21st – Quiet day. Slight shelling – Ground in Front was reconnoitred – Quiet night. Rain fell. Capt & Acting G.H.WALLIS DCM. intends to relieve knocked conveying supplies to Battalion was wounded by Shell. Died of wounds 21.st	
"	21st		See Report on Operations – Casualties Officers Killed - Captain E.W. BETHELL. Lieut H.L.C. WHITTAKER. Lieut M.B. BLAGDEN. 2ndLt R.F. HIGGS 32nd. Wounded Captain K.A.BROWN 2nd Bn. Died of wounds 22nd. Lieut W.G.PRATT. M.M. Lieut T.BROOKSBYSR. D.C.M. ?R.SM Lieut J.G.HARKER S.Yeo attached.	AppD 168. 169
	22nd			

WAR DIARY
INTELLIGENCE SUMMARY

1st Batt. THE QUEENS Regt.

SEPTEMBER 1918

Army Form C. 2118.

Place	Date	Hour	Summary of Events and Information	Remarks and references to Appendices
	22		Wounded remained at duty — Lieut P.J. JAKES M.M. Other ranks Killed 39. Wounded 184. Missing 89.	
		4 pm	Orders received Lieut Col P.C. ESDAILE was to proceed to B. Echelon Major G.K. OLIVER M.C. to assume temporary command of Battn. Orders for relief by 2nd Battn Warwickshire Regt brought receive about 7 pm. Fn. 0170 Relief commenced about 8.45 pm. completed 1.30 hrs. On relief Coys marched independently to trenches in V.17 a — move completed	
V.17 a	23rd		at 4.15am R. Hot meal was in waiting for the troops. Troops rested till noon when cleaning up and refitting was proceeded with.	
	24th		Training and general routine — refitting proceeded with. Lieut S.G.W. HUNT (M.C.) to England with time expired to W.O.	
	25		Training and general routine — 330 O.R. Minimum Reserve exchanged — Lt Col P.C. ESDAILE and Lieut J.S. MILNER under instruction from 10th proceeded to Roeplan Camp BLEAKENCOURT to await further instructions	

WAR DIARY

INTELLIGENCE SUMMARY

Army Form C. 2118.

SEPTEMBER 1918. 4th Battn Middlesex Regt

Place	Date	Hour	Summary of Events and Information	Remarks and references to Appendices
V.17.a.	26		Training and general routine. Orders received Bn to move forward at 7pm forward to CAVALRY TRENCH and CAVALRY SUPPORT. Trench were reconnoitred by 2/Lieut J.E. SHIPTON and 1 N.C.O. guide from each Coy and H.Q. Move cancelled. Lieut H. MALLETT assumed command of "C" Company.	
"	27		Captain R.H. PHILPOT M.C. assumed command of "B" Coy on instruction from Brigade. Captain H.G. IRESON R.A.M.C. ordered to join 18th Middlesex Regt (Morteros). Lieut A.C. PATTERSON R.A.M.C. joined and assumed medical charge of Battalion. On instructions from Bde C and A Coys moved forward of Battalion - or instructions from Bde Captain V.S. BINGHAM, M.C. moved forward C & A Coys to occupy CAVALRY TRENCH & Coy CAVALRY SUPPORT - Remainder of Battn to move forward at 7pm to ROCKET TRENCH. Battn H.Q. VAUCELETTE FARM. Move complete 10.30pm.	
X.13.c.	28		A & C Coys "B" H.Q. moved from ROCKET TRENCH VAUCELETTE FARM to CAVALRY SUPPORT TRENCH. Coy Commanders reconnoitred the ground front S. of VILLERS GUISLAIN in preparation for an advance.	

WAR DIARY or **INTELLIGENCE SUMMARY**
Army Form C. 2118.

SEPTEMBER 1918
PAGE 9
1st Bn. The Queen's Regt.

Place	Date	Hour	Summary of Events and Information	Remarks
WIBd	29		Battalion at half an hour notice to move. "B" Coy at 3 p.m. ordered to take up position in CAVALRY TRENCH & cover rally S. of CHAPEL STREET in case enemy attacked. Ho detached from VILLERS GUISLAIN. Move completed at 4 p.m. Attack from a few shells dropped on outside B. HQrs. The prisoners we & from trenches were put into our hut. WA NORTH slightly had they were not gas shells. In echo were removed - later it transpired that the shells had contained gas & D Coy was much further north along the trenches. The shell hole were treated with chloride of lime & placed in Gibraltar. 2 other ranks wounded.	
	30		At 'stand to' in the morning the gas shells of the previous day took effect chiefly affecting the eyes & during the day the following were admitted to hospital Lieut H. MALLETT, 2/Lt R. HAGGARD, WA NORTH, 2nd Lt J. E. SHIPTON & W.J.C. MORGAN, & Lieut A.C. PATTERSON (R.A.M.C.) the M.O. and 139 other ranks. At 6 pm. the Commanding Officer Major G.K. OLLIVER M.C. received orders from the Brigadier General Commdg.	

WAR DIARY or INTELLIGENCE SUMMARY

SEPTEMBER 1918   Army Form C. 2118.

1st Bn The Queen's Regt   PAGE 10

Place	Date	Hour	Summary of Events and Information	Remarks and references to Appendices
W.18.d.	30		to proceed to 33rd Divisional Reception Camp + handing over the command of the battalion to Capt R.H. PHILPOT M.C. Capt S.E. ACHPITEL M.C. assumed command of "B" Coy. During the afternoon 2/Lt T. RUDKIN + A.E. SAUNDERS reconnoitred the route to THORSTAUERRY no orders had been received that the battalion would probably move there. 2/Lt E.A. FIELD took over the duties of Lewis gun officer from 2/Lt W.J.C. MORGAN. Lieut R.M. EAST took over the duties of Adjutant from 2/Lt J.E. SHIPTON. "D" Coy having supplied its Lewis gun Coy this owing to the fact "C" Coy + "D" Coy were amalgamated under the command of Capt E.S. BINGHAM M.C. "B" Echelon moved to W.17.d.	

T.W.F. Report. Capt
Comdg 1st Bn The Queens Regt

WAR DIARY
INTELLIGENCE SUMMARY

Army Form C. 2118.

OCTOBER R/1/18

1/Bn The Queens Regt RWS

Place	Date	Hour	Summary of Events and Information	Remarks and references to Appendices
M18a3d	1		Improvement of trenches occupied & mentioned antril	
	2		Morning. Enquiry not from 0900 hrs to 1200 hrs. Orders received that the 19th Bn wired relieve the 90th Bn in the left sector in Orc pool on nights 2/3rd. The battalion would not have to be relieved for relief a battalion of the 101st Bde on nights 3rd/4th. 2/Lts C.S.CLARK & W.R.RODLAND joined him quarters from the Base.	
	3		Enemy carried out from 10 00 hrs to 13 00 hrs A/12 who Verbal notice received that Battn moved to forward zone at 14 00 hrs BN 13 who even occurred that battalion would relieve 2nd Bn The Winesh in frm Regt in Bn Support. Battalion marched off at 14 15 hrs. Relief complete at 18 25 hrs. Dispositions of Battalion	B.O.199

WAR DIARY or INTELLIGENCE SUMMARY

OCTOBER 1918

1st Bn. The Queen's Regt.

Army Form C. 2118.

Page 2

Place	Date	Hour	Summary of Events and Information	Remarks and references to Appendices
W18A29.	3		"A" Coy in trenches near TYHURST QUARRY - "B" Coy in trench between TYHURST QUARRY & KILDARE AVENUE in T23a. "C" Coy in PIGEON TRENCH in T23a6. 1 casualty 2/Lt P.H.E. WHITTAKER. S.H. PIERSSENE - F. ESPROSTON - H.C. CRAWLEY and Pte MOULTRIE joined the Battalion from the base & went to minimum Reserve.	
T26 & 80.	4		A very quiet day. A little gas shelling at night. Orders received for discharge wired. The fire battery 12.10 hrs 10300 (55) (N) the Bn who cancelled. stated O. JACKMAN. M.M. joined minimum Reserve from the Base.	
	5		Orders received that 19th Bn were to be handed to one another of our Line from PUTNEY to the ST. QUENTIN CANAL. Detached Coy Line from PUTNEY to	

WAR DIARY or INTELLIGENCE SUMMARY

Army Form C. 2118.

PAGE 3

OCTOBER 1918

1/B The Queens Regt

Place	Date	Hour	Summary of Events and Information	Remarks and references to Appendices

X22 c-80 5 KINGSTON QUARRY from threes to S.2.C. The Cameronians and 1st Scottish Rifles moved away thro' and the Battalion remained in support. At 13.45 hrs telephone orders were received that Battalion would move to trenches running north to S.15.n. Vestrl. Orders issued to Coys. leading Company "C" moved off at 14.20 hrs followed by "B", "A" & "D" Btn Hdqrs.

TARGELLE ROAD — LOCK N B.D.B. Three assembly country to S.15.a. Coys disposed — A Coy in trench from S.15.a.2.3 to S.15.a.4.3. B Coy from S.15.a.4 to 3.6 S.15.a.7.4.(in trench) C Coy in trench from S.15.a.7.4 to S.15.c.6.26. Move complete at 15.25 hrs. Rest O.V. Bernard arrived from leave & took over duties of Signalling Officer.

S.14.6.60 6 Improvement of the trenches observed that the 19* Bde are very proud of the 32nd Division would help trench with the 38th Div. who were in front & conform to

19* Bde are very proud of the 32nd Division

WAR DIARY

INTELLIGENCE SUMMARY

OCTOBER 1918

1/Bn The Queens Rgt

Army Form C. 2118. Page 4.

Place	Date	Hour	Summary of Events and Information	Remarks and references to Appendices
Siège 82	6		An advance made by Btns. 1/Col. H. H. Lee D.S.O. (?) The Emergency arrived with orders comprised of the Battalion from Capt R.W. Philpot M.C. Capt N.B. Avery rejoined minimum Reserve from Senior Officers Course at Aldershot. B Echelon moved to S.20.a.	
"	7		A + C Coys found a working party to repair roads. Capt. R.W. Philpot M.C. proceeded to join minimum Reserve. 2nd Lts. E.A. Saunders, N. Bassett + J.A. Crookes proceeded to minimum Reserve preparatory to going to Senior Officers School. Their places were taken by 2/Lts. J.C. Crawley, C.S. Clark + W.B. Rutland.	
"	8		Training carried out from 09.00 hrs. to 12.00 hrs. At 17.00 hrs. telephone orders received that Battalion would move to	

WAR DIARY
INTELLIGENCE SUMMARY

Army Form C. 2118.

OCTOBER 1918.

PAGE 5.

1/6 Bn. The Queens Regt.

Place	Date	Hour	Summary of Events and Information	Remarks and references to Appendices
S.14.B.2	8		LA PANNERIE NORTH (S16.d.Q.4.) Concentrate there & be prepared to move at very short notice - Battalion moved off at 17.15 hrs accompanied by a train line. Complete at 18.30 hrs. The battalion bivouacked in the open at 21.45 hrs. Orders were received that the battalion would move forward to take the line of the road running N.W. & S.E. in 01 c & d at 05.20 hrs. and that operations might be expected as soon as this was done.	
S.16.a.9.4.	9		Battalion moved off at 04.45 hrs and marched through AUBENCHEUL-AUX-BOIS & VILLERS OUTREAUX, at T.10 central. It was found the road had been mined & that it was impossible to get transport any further. Lewis guns were unloaded & march continued through MALINCOURT its Battalion arriving & preparing H position for the advance at 05.10 hrs.	A.D.201

OCTOBER 1918.

Army Form C. 2118.

PAGE 6.

WAR DIARY
or
INTELLIGENCE SUMMARY.
(Erase heading not required.)

1st Bn The Queens Regt

Place	Date	Hour	Summary of Events and Information	Remarks and references to Appendices
O29 B4.	9		See report on operations attached. Casualties Capt A.R. ABERCROMBIE OBE wounded, 3 O.Ranks killed 16 O.R wounded. Barnes Copse 25. Transport moved to HIPPERS OUTPOST. Minimum Reserve to same place. 2/Lt J RICE joined Maximum Reserve from the Base.	See Report
P2 d 96.	10		At 12.00 hrs Battalion moved into Factory at P3 d 9.6. with B. HQ in the same place. Batchelor moved to P.7.d. 2/Lt E.L. PHILLIPS joined. Minimum Reserve (who had moved to VILLER au BERTRY) from Base.	
P3 d 96.	11		Baths were improvised, all men Batted, relieved up. Evening carried out from 10.00 hrs to 12.00 hrs.	

(A9029) W: W2358/P360 60,000 12/17 D. D. & L. Sch. 52a. Forms/C2118/15.

WAR DIARY
INTELLIGENCE SUMMARY

Army Form C. 2118.

PAGE 7

OCTOBER 1918

2nd Bn. The Queens Regt.

Place	Date	Hour	Summary of Events and Information	Remarks and references to Appendices
Pbgb	12		News received that Battalion would move into billets at MALINCOURT. Battalion paraded & marched off at 11.00 hrs via cross country tracks & more via Coulette at 14.10 hrs. On completion of move Minimum Reserve rejoined the Battalion. 2/Lt T. H. MAYLAND joined the Battalion from the Base, 2/Lts Maspel & Bachelor rejoined the Battalion.	2nd Bn
MALINCOURT TS.80.15	13		At 10.15 hrs the Battalion was inspected on parade at T.5.a by the Divisional Commander Maj. Gen. Sir R. T. PINNEY K.C.B. who afterwards addressed it & congratulated the Battalion on their advance of the 9th inst.	
"	14		Training and General Routine.	

WAR DIARY
INTELLIGENCE SUMMARY

OCTOBER 1918.

Army Form C. 2118.

Page 8

Pte. He Queens Regt.

Place	Date	Hour	Summary of Events and Information	Remarks and references to Appendices
MALINCOURT	15		Training and General Routine. Inspection inspected by the Brig General commanding the 19th Bde. who gave a good report.	
"	16		Training and General Routine.	
"	17		" " " Lieut J. TALBOT with 50 O.R.- Re-inforcements joined Battalion from England.	
"	18		Training and General Routine. Bn Exercise without troops took place - Company Officers and Company Commanders took part. Orders received Brigade would march to TROISVILLES on 19th inst.	
"	19		Battalion marched to TROISVILLES by cross country tracks arriving at village of CLARY and BERTRY - move completed by 2 pm. Battalion quartered in billets. C.O. Adjt and Coy Cmdrs took part in a Reconnaissance	En. D. 2.c.8

WAR DIARY / INTELLIGENCE SUMMARY

1st Batt "The Queens"
OCTOBER 1918
Army Form C. 2118.
Page 9

Place	Date	Hour	Summary of Events and Information	Remarks and references to Appendices
TROISVILLES	20		Lieut K.M. EKET to Batt H.Q. temporary D/S as 2nd Staff Captain. General Routine — Light Training, special attention being given to Coy. Manoeuvres — Nature of operation it is probable the Battalion will be called on to carry out in the near future. A number of N.Y. shells fell in and around the village during the night. No casualties. Lieut P.J. JAKES. M.M. & Bar. H.Q. 1st Battn. Scout officer.	
"	21		General Routine and Light Training as on 20th Lieut C.P. MILES D.S.O. "THE CAMERONIANS" proceeded to take over command of 1st Batt. to CAMERONIANS." Lieut Col Hon. H. RITCHIE D.S.O. Scottish Rifles assumed command of 1st Bn. Major P.C. ESDAILE to P.B. Employ of army. 15th Capt G.R. OLLIVER M.C. to 6th Batt. 2nd Lieut J.S. MILNER to England — report to War office — 21st one Truck off the strength of Battalion. Orders received Batt. will take part in forthcoming connected with advance of 3rd and 4th Armies. Battalion to move to overnight Mr. O. DOS Position in 57C. K6 a. 2 in the evening. Field SHERWOOD and PIGGINS E. Seriously injured	
"	22		General Routine — Fitting out — Inspection to prior to going into Battle Cards conveying congratulations by Maj Gen. Sir R.J. Pinney K.C.B. 1st Canadian reserve for and manual to 144739 Cpl S. TUCKER and 39833 L/C J. FERN.	

WAR DIARY or **INTELLIGENCE SUMMARY**
(Erase heading not required.)

OCTOBER 1918   Army Form C. 2118.

7/1 Batt. The Queen's Reg.

Place	Date	Hour	Summary of Events and Information	Remarks and references to Appendices
N.E of LE CATEAU	Night 22nd &		Battalion engaged in Active Operations	See Report An.O.209
	26th		On completion of Special operation carried out by the Battalion N.E. of ENGLEFONTAINE on morning of 26th Troops were withdrawn to outskirts of POIX du NORD – Relieved by 27th R.W.F. 26th Division 5 p.m. Company marched independently to FOREST where hot tea was served – after about one hours the march to TROISVILLES was continued as a Battalion – men were completed and troops in billets by midnight one man only was unable to complete the march. Capt F.C. CHUBB. H. MALLETT. a/Lieut. L. WALKER. – S. JONES invalided to England – Chief of strength – Draft of 159 O.R from England joined on Batt.	
TROISVILLES	27		General Routine - Refitting. etc. Major (A/Lt Colt) H.H.GREEN DSO. The Buffs joined and assumed command of Battalion.	
	28		Training and General Routine	

WAR DIARY

OCTOBER 1918

INTELLIGENCE SUMMARY 1st Batt. The Queen's Regt.

Army Form C. 2118.

Place	Date	Hour	Summary of Events and Information	Remarks and references to Appendices
TROISVILLES	29		Training and general routine. Lieut A.J.R. HAGGARD reported from Hospital on recovering from wound (gas). Captain R.H. PHILPOT M.C. ceased to act as major in H.Q. and took over command of "C" Coy. Captain N.B. AVERY M.C. from "C" Coy joined Batln. H.Q. and assumed duties of Senior Major. Draft of 36 O.R. joined from England.	
"	30		Training and general routine. Apps... who inspected by Corps Commander.	
"	31		Training and general routine.	

H.C. Green Lieut. Colonel
Comdg 1st Batt. The Queen's Regt

WAR DIARY
INTELLIGENCE SUMMARY

NOVEMBER 1918 Army Form C. 2118.
1st Batt. 7th Queen's Regt.

Vol 49

Place	Date	Hour	Summary of Events and Information	Remarks and references to Appendices
TROISVILLES	1st		Training and general routine. Multiple received 23823 L/C S.H.EDEN awarded the 6 M.M. and 14439 Cpl S.TUCKER awarded M.M. Gazettes M.M./M.M. 9 October 1918 (Authy Cpl M.M. 3115/6 of 22.10.18).	3H 1/RWS
"	2		Training and general routine —	
"	3		Divine Service held in open just W. of Church. Bn. received Battalion to move with Brigade to assembly area E. of POIX au NORD on 4th instant in connection with operations commencing on that date.	
"	4		Battalion less Lewis Gunners Reserved) moved off 11.15 hrs and marched through MONTAY thence across country to ENGLEFONTAINE where the Bn went into billets. Orders were received that the Bn would pass through the 98th Inf Bde and occupy high ground W. of AULNOYE STATION (sheets 5/45?) from U.28.a.16. — C.4.a. 95.80, and there in conjunction with 5/S.R.	

WAR DIARY
INTELLIGENCE SUMMARY

Army Form C. 2118.

NOVEMBER 1918

1st Bn. The Queens Regt.

Page 2

Place	Date	Hour	Summary of Events and Information	Remarks and references to Appendices
ENGLEFONTAINE	4th		Took direct hit 9 km behind around AULNOYE STATION (Sheet No 51. U29). Remainr. Reserve proceeded to billets in FOREST.	
"	5th		(Capt a/Maj W.B. Avery M.C. & Lieut A.J.R. Haggard c/to 06.00 hours the Battalion moved via HECQ along ROUTE D'HECQ — LES GRANDES PATURES to a point 5a 6.6 in the FORET DE MORMAL where the battalion bivouacked for the night. Orders were received that the 19th Bde. would become the advanced guard to the 33rd Division & take up an outpost position on high ground east of MAUBERGE – AVESNES road, the battalion forming part of the main body of the Advanced Guard. Orders received that the battalion would advance across the River SAMBRE & pass through the 5th Scottish Rifles on high ground in U.28 the the village in U.29 and consolidate on road from U.30.a. 4.7. to Cross roads U.30.c 6.6.	
B 5a 6.6	6th		At 11.00 hours battalion moved off & crossed the SAMBRE & employed east of the River. The battalion attached 4 tanks their Section & were on operation attached with 21st Division & left & the Cameronians on the right. See report Casualties 10. R&R Killed 10. R&h Missing 2. O.R&h wounded. Prisoners taken 13. Transport moved to a field U.25c (sheet 51). About 23.00 hours battalion received orders that the S.S.R. would pass through them at 05.45 hours the following morning to take the line of the villages ECHELIN POT DE VIN. The battalion to follow 1000 yds which the S.S.R. attain their objective. The battalion Riflemen arrange the after they had taken line on high ground east of MAUBERGE – AVESNES Road.	See report Appendix 1

WAR DIARY or INTELLIGENCE SUMMARY

Army Form C. 2118.

NOVEMBER 1918

1st Bn. "The Queen's" Regt. Page 3

Place	Date	Hour	Summary of Events and Information	Remarks and references to Appendices
ALLNOYE STATION	6th		Transport moved to a field in U.25.d. Medical turned to England + struck off the strength of the Battalion.	On Report
"	7th		Owing to thick mist the 5th Scottish Rifles moved to Battalion except to one company which went through at 6.45. The Battalion moved forward in artillery formation A + B Coys still leading with C + D in support. The Battalion took village of ECUELIN + found his east of the village. The Battalion reported strong opposition was encountered on entering the village. Separate report attached. Village was cleared by 09.20 hours. Casualties 2/Lieut O. JACKMAN wounded. Capt R. H. NEVINS M.C. Lieut F.W. M.M. killed. Lt. Col. A.W.J. REEN. D.S.O. 5 O.Ranks killed. FELLING 2/Lieut F.H.E. WHITTAKER wounded 6 O.Ranks missing. 43 O.Ranks wounded. AULNOYE STATION to field in U.30.a, where through village transport was shelled 4 horses killed 2 horses wounded. At 20.00 hours verbal orders received that the Battalion would be relieved by 13th Welsh Regt. By night. Relief completed at 02.00 hours on 8th. Battalion moved by Coys to LA TOQUE. Len coy arriving at 07.45 hrs and the Battalion was there for remainder of night moved to SARBARAS. Transport joined Battalion. At 16.30 hrs Battalion accompanied	See Report Appendix 1
ECUELIN	8th			

WAR DIARY

INTELLIGENCE SUMMARY.

NOVEMBER 1918 Army Form C. 2118.

PAGE 4

1st Bn The Queen's Regt.

Place	Date	Hour	Summary of Events and Information	Remarks and references to Appendices
BERLIAMONT	8.		by the Transport marched to BERLIAMONT and billeted. Minimum Reserve joined Bn. at SARBARAS. Capt (a/Maj) N. BAVERY, M.C., assumed command of the Bn. Capt. R.H. PHILPOT, M.C., took over the appointment of Major on Bn M.O. Lieut A.J.R. HAGGARD that of Actg. Adjt.	
-"-	9.		General routine. Cleaning up kit & Tillets inspections.	
-"-	10.		Bn. paraded for Divine Service at 10-30 hours. Notification of the award of the M.M. to men of the Bn received.	See attd. App. 2.
-"-	11.		News of Germany's acceptance of the Allies Armistice Terms received 0835 hrs. With the exception of necessary routine no work was done on this day. 1/3 O.RKs joined Bn. from Base.	
-"-	12.		Baths were allotted to Battn. from 0900 k 1200 hours. A further draft of 11 O.Rks joined Bn.	

WAR DIARY or INTELLIGENCE SUMMARY

Army Form C. 2118.

NOVEMBER 1918

1st Bn. Middlesex Regt.

PAGE 5

Place	Date	Hour	Summary of Events and Information	Remarks and references to Appendices
BERLIAMONT	13		Companies at disposal of O.C's Coys for reorganisation. One hours close order drill carried out. I.G. classes commenced. Many congratulatory telegrams received from higher formation. The recent reinforcements were inspected by C.O. 19th Inf. Bde.	
	14		Training general routine. Orders for move KLOCQUIGNOL received. Notification of the award of the MM to 5 O.R. of the Bn.	App 2. B.O. 222.
			Preparing for move KLOCQUIGNOL issued.	
	15		Bn paraded at 09.45 and marched KLOCQUIGNOL. Movement complete by 12.35 hrs. Thanks T.E. SHIPTON deferred. Orders received for move to FOREST. Bn return issued.	B.O. 223
	16		Bn paraded at 09.00 and marched to FOREST. Move was complete by 13.25 hrs. Orders received for move to	

WAR DIARY
INTELLIGENCE SUMMARY

NOVEMBER 1918 PAGE 7
1st Bn "Hallucina" Regt.

Place	Date	Hour	Summary of Events and Information	Remarks and references to Appendices
	16 (cont)		CLARY. Bn. Orders issued for move.	BO 224
	17.		Bn marched to CLARY. Move was completed by 1300 hrs. The following officers joined Bn. from England. A/Cpl "Hume" 2/Lt TINDALL 2 Bn, 2/Lt T WARD + 2/Lt STRINGER 2 Bn. 2/Lt AK FAIRLIE 2/Lts AE MAILEY + REK ROBERTS. Capt + Q.M. W BOOKER. 2/Lt Henwood Foresta join Bn to up appointment Q.O.M. Lieut A. T. R. HAGGARD assumed temporary command of "A" Coy. 2/Lieut J. F. SHIPTON appointed Actg. Adjt.	
	18.		Training general routine	
	19.		The Bde C. inspected Billets. Interviewed newly joined Officers. Training + general routine.	

WAR DIARY
INTELLIGENCE SUMMARY
(Erase heading not required.)

NOVEMBER 1918 Army Form C. 2118.
1st Bn Mullenin Rgh PAGE 8

Place	Date	Hour	Summary of Events and Information	Remarks and references to Appendices
CLARY	20		Training & general routine. 2/Lieuts F. RAWLINSON and A.T. GREENAWAY joined the Bn and were posted to A & B Coys respectively. Lieut A. FAIRLIE was transferred to D Coy. Baths have been allotted 4th Bn from 13-00 till 19-00 hrs. All men were bathed except D Coy. [illegible]	
	21		Training & general routine. The R.C. inspected the transport at 10:30 hrs. The Bn formed up Mass for Bn Drill at 11:00 hrs.	
	22		Training & general routine. The advance party for CORBIE area proceeded lorry at 07:45 hrs. Lieut BN A. IONIDES joined the Bn and was posted to B Coy. Lieut D. Burrow returned from hospital.	

WAR DIARY

INTELLIGENCE SUMMARY. 10t-3rd Bn "Fusiliers" Rgt.

NOVEMBER 1918 — PAGE 9

Place	Date	Hour	Summary of Events and Information	Remarks and references to Appendices
CLARY	23		The Bn. was employed in salving old Brigade Salvage Area. A further Burial party of 1 NCO for CoY was despatched to the CORBIE area at 0745 hours.	
	24		The Bn. paraded at 11.05 hours and marched to fill 300x S.of village where a Thanksgiving and Memorial Service was held. This service included all denominations except R.Cs. The SM. MONCROFT, M.C. & H.S. SAVAGE joined the Bn.	
	25		The Bn. Route march arranged for today was cancelled owing to rain. A Lecture was given by Capt. G.F. Ashpitel M.C. on 'Emigration' at 1100 hrs.	

… NOVEMBER 1918 Army Form C. 2118. PAGE 10
1/3 Bn Thulluwia Regt.

WAR DIARY
INTELLIGENCE SUMMARY
(Erase heading not required.)

Place	Date	Hour	Summary of Events and Information	Remarks and references to Appendices
CLARY	26		Parade march detailed for 2nd took place. There were no mentioning out 2/Lieuts. A.C. BATTSON, R.O. ANTHONY and H.C. ALLEN, M.M. from R.W. Kent Regt. joined Bn from Base. A lecture was given at the Divn Recreation Room by th Rev. S. KENNEDY on "Bimbashed". Notification received of award of the Military Cross to 3 Officers of th Bn.	Full particulars
	27		Lieut (A/Capt) R.H.M.BROCK M.C. joins the Bn. Training continued routine samme out	
	28		The R.S.C. Inspects the Regtl Transport. Notification received of forthcoming Cycles at 10-o-clrs move from present area	

WAR DIARY
INTELLIGENCE SUMMARY.— 1st Bn The Queen's Regt

NOVEMBER 1918 Army Form C. 2118.

PAGE 11.

Place	Date	Hour	Summary of Events and Information	Remarks and references to Appendices
CLARY	29.		The Brigade Ceremonial Parade arranged for today was cancelled owing to the weather. Training in coy areas and general routine carried out.	
"	30		Training and general Routine carried out. The Inter Platoon Rugby Football competition was played off. Platoon No. 6.2 after an exciting game won by 3 goals to nil. Major S.T. WATSON D.S.O. and O.M.Lt. ROUTLEY joined the Bn. 6 local miners were despatched to CAMBRAI prior to transfer to England. 7 NCO's provided to the Base Depot en route for England on leave.	

M.B. Strong, Major
Comdg 1st Bn The Queen's Regt

WAR DIARY
or
INTELLIGENCE SUMMARY. 1st Bn Wellington Regt.

DECEMBER 1918 Army Form C. 2118.

351/R005

Place	Date	Hour	Summary of Events and Information	Remarks and references to Appendices
CAIRO	1		A party of 3 Argylls and A Coy under 2/Lt [?] England on exchange. "H" Bn paraded at 10:45 hrs for quinine issue, which was held in the Cinema.	
	2		A column party consisting of Capt. R.H. Pepper M.C., 2nd Lt H Barrett Munn, 1 S/M, 1 W.O., 1 Cpl/sgt and 6 selected from paraded to Boulogne en route for ENGLAND filled the King and the Rugt Colours	
	3		"A" Bn route marched for lasting 2 hours 20 minutes. There was no rifle falling out. 'H' Bn played 7 [?] at football winning by goals to 1.	
	4		Troops returned routine carried out until 11 o'clock at 11.35 Bn handed and marched to [?] where they were formed up on mass	

WAR DIARY
or
INTELLIGENCE SUMMARY.
(Erase heading not required.)

Army Form C. 2118.
DECEMBER 1918
1st Bn The Queen's Regt
PAGE 2

Place	Date	Hour	Summary of Events and Information	Remarks and references to Appendices
CLARY	4(contd)		with the Officers jumped just clear of the road. At about 12.25 hrs. H.M. The King drove past in his car on his way from ELINCOURT to LIGNY and was heartily cheered.	
"	5		Baths were allotted to the Bn. today. A training programme was issued previously. Coy's of their Bn.ANTHONY and borne bringing KEAVEUIL where a staying camp for the more of the troops to the War area is provided.	
"	5(cont)		A march of 1 hr. + 3 M.M. received training in M.T. small arms L.G.Chace carried out firing practice. Platoon played on the square.	
"	6		The Bn. paraded at 0910 hrs for a route march when late, about 2½ hours - there was no incident and The Bgde. Transport were inspected by Lt. Lt. R. G.P.E.E. CMGD.SO.	

WAR DIARY / INTELLIGENCE SUMMARY

December 1918 — 10th Bn. Shillwine Regt.

Army Form C. 2118. PAGE 3

Place	Date	Hour	Summary of Events and Information	Remarks and references to Appendices
CLARY	6 (contd)		Arrival of 3 M.M's received.	App 1
"	7		Training & general routine. Arrival of the Rugby team. Played 5th Bn. The Loyals Regt. at football losing 0-3. The Rugby team played 7th Bn. Shillwine Regt. losing by 8 pts to 12.	
"	8		The Bn. played parade for Divine Service at 10:00hr marching to the CINEMA Hippo where the Service was held. The Drums played in the square during the afternoon. Two Courts of Enquiry & one received.	
"	9		Training. Received notices kept KM & Col returned Bn from England. Orders for move to MASNIERS and Standing Orders for those received from Brigade Bn Standing Orders returns for march.	D.R.O. B.O. 253
"	10		MASNIERS reached.	

WAR DIARY or INTELLIGENCE SUMMARY

Army Form C. 2118.

1st Bn Influenia Regt PAGE 4
DECEMBER 1918

Place	Date	Hour	Summary of Events and Information	Remarks and references to Appendices
CLARY	10.		The Bn. transmo entrained at MASNIERES. Entraining station from 1150 & 1300 hrs for dinner.	
MASNIERES			On arrival Bn. was quartered in factory on W. outskirts. Willage Bn Orders received. Bn Order transmo'd to HERMIES. Issued. Arrival of 1 Bn. R.M.C., 1 M.C.), 11 D.C.M. received.	BO 258 APP 1
—	11.		The Bn marched on march to HERMIES.	
HERMIES			Movement completed by 1250 hrs. Arrival Bn was quartered in Huts. Nothing abnormal. Nil. Bn Orders for march FAVREUIL issued. Bn Orders BO 259 published.	BO 259
—	13.		The Bn transmo marched to FAVREUIL. Entraining station from 1150 & 1730 hrs for dinner. Movement completed by hrs. 1030 hrs. In ordinary Bn Orders received. march — ONE Bn. de Ordres received Bn Orders formed	

WAR DIARY DECEMBER 1918 Army Form C. 2118.
or
INTELLIGENCE SUMMARY. 10/R Fullness R.F. PAGE 5
(Erase heading not required.)

Place	Date	Hour	Summary of Events and Information	Remarks and references to Appendices
FAVREUIL	13(cont)		to ALBERT march.	3028
- -	14		Bufrand advanced march with whole	
ALBERT			from 1150 K 1300hrs ALBERT arrived. Bn. in quarters in a camp on N.E. edge town. Messing complete by two Notably at Mr Bee. Orders for march QUERRIEU area received. Bn. Hdqrs. 30259 carried.	
- -	15		Bufnd. advance will resumed. Bn. halt from 1150 K 1300hrs to ALLONVILLE M.C. was completed by 1550 hrs. Notably out Nil B. was qtred in village. Bttl. hdn. in Chateau. 100ª E of Church. Billeting for night at ST. SAUVEUR	
ALLONVILLE			area issued. Brigade orders.	3028

WAR DIARY
INTELLIGENCE SUMMARY
(Erase heading not required.)

Army Form C. 2118.

DECEMBER 1918 1st/8th Wellington Rgt. PAGE 6

Place	Date	Hour	Summary of Events and Information	Remarks and references to Appendices
ABONVILLE	16		Battalion ad marched with the	
BREILLY			usual Gnison halts to BREILLY-Sur-SOMME.	
			MOS 6/50 complete by 1400 hrs. Notably on a	
			march - Nil. Btn transport motor fine	
			Instructions received Bn trans for march	
			CAMPS L'AMIENOIS and HALLEVILLERS tomorrow	BO.6
—	17		Battalion again on march but with usual	
			Gnison halts. CAMPS and HALLEVILLERS,	
			Bn HQ and A+B Coys understand to CAMPS C+D Coys	
			to HALLEVILLERS. Moves complete by 1400 hrs	
			Notably on march. Th Adv Party reported the Bn	
CAMPS	18		The Coys were spent cleaning up billets kit etc	
			and in filling up many facilities for utilising	
			was found that the inhabitants in this area it	
			amount of kit was given	

WAR DIARY
or
INTELLIGENCE SUMMARY.
(Erase heading not required.)

DECEMBER 1918 Army Form C. 2113.
1st Bn Shropshire L.I.

Place	Date	Hour	Summary of Events and Information	Remarks and references to Appendices
CAMPS	19		Continuation of cleaning up and preparation of billets for troops.	
	20		Training opened. Routine.	
	21		Training opened. Routine. Clean clothes issued.	
	22		A divine service was held in Rex Richenbas Room CAMPS at 0900 hrs. Lieut Col R Bellamy DSO 1st Royal Sussex Regt. joined the Bn. and assumed command from this date. General Routine.	
	23		Baths were allotted to this Bn. all ranks. Very Indian.	

WAR DIARY
or
INTELLIGENCE SUMMARY.
(Erase heading not required.)

Army Form C. 2118.
DECEMBER 1918
PAGE 8
10th Influence Rgt.

Place	Date	Hour	Summary of Events and Information	Remarks and references to Appendices
CAMPS	25		Companies celebrated Xmas. Greetings Received the G.O.C. 33rd Divn & 119 Bde wished the Bn. in person a Good Xmas. Sergeants & Officers Dinner O.R. B 2.30 PM. Other Ranks were the Guests of the Officers today.	
"	26		Special Orders of the day by the G.O.C. received Authorizing the Xmas flight of H.M. The King, H.M. the Queen and those of Field Marshal Sir Haig the Xmas Dinner of A.& C. Companies held today.	
"	27		Transport Mens dinner. Training & General Routine carried out.	
"	28		Owing to bad weather Route March had to be abandoned. Training in billets carried out.	

WAR DIARY
INTELLIGENCE SUMMARY
1st Bn. The Queen's Regt.
DECEMBER 1918

Army Form C. 2118.
PAGE 9

Place	Date	Hour	Summary of Events and Information	Remarks and references to Appendices
CAMPS	29		The Bn. less C in C troops paraded for Divine Service in Church Army Marquee on Bn's Football Ground at 0930 hrs.	
"	30		Training & General Routine. Notification of probable move to men and attachment to 98th L.T. Bn. received. Entraining strength wired to Bde.	
"	31		The Transport was inspected by the Bde. C. on new MIRAINES - POIX Rd in the village of CAMPS. Warning order for move to HAVRE received.	

R. Blacker
Lieut. Col.
Comdg. 1st Bn. The Queen's Regt.

SECRET Battalion Orders No 255
by Major R. B. Avery M.C.
Commanding 3rd The Queens Regt.

14

December 10th 1918

Detail for tomorrow
   Subaltern of the day   2/Lieut D.E. MOTLEY

Ref: MAP, VALENCIENNES 1/100,000.

1. The Battalion will parade in order H.Q, A, B, Drums, C, D, ready to move off at 09.00 hrs tomorrow 11th & will march to MASNIERES distance about 11 miles.

2. Particular attention is called to Battn Standing Orders for this move, previously issued 1 copy per recipient of Battn Orders.

3. Starting point :- Cross Roads ½ mile E.S.E. of Y in CAULLERY Battn H.Q. will pass this point at 09.12 hrs.

4. Route :- LIGNY - HAUCOURT - ESNES - LESDAIN - GREVECOURT.

5. The following distances will be maintained on the march.
   500 yds between Battalions
   100 "   "   Companies
   100 "   "   Units & its transport
   50   "   "   each section of 12 vehicles

6. Compasses & maps will be carried by all Officers possessing them.

7. There will be a halt from 11.50 hrs to 13.00 hrs for dinners - Cookers will therefore march in rear of their respective Companies.

8. 2/Lieut F.T.F. MOULTRIE is detailed as Billeting Officer, Billeting party as laid down will parade at O.Room at 07.15 hrs. Battn Sig Officer will arrange that bicycles are ready at that hour. This party will proceed to MASNIERES reporting to the Staff Captain at the CHURCH at 09.30 hrs.

9. The Battn Sig. Officer will arrange for synchronisation of watches before 08.30 hrs.

10. Blankets will be ready for loading at times as under :-
    H.Q, A & B. Companies at respective H.Qrs at 07.15 hr
    C & D Companies at Q.M. Stores by 07.30 hrs
    Jerkins in bundles of 10 & labelled will be ready for loading at Q.M. stores by 07.15 hrs.
    Valises will be at R.Q.M. stores by 08.00 hrs
    Officers Mess Basket at O. Mess at 08.15 hrs

11. On 12th inst. Battalion will march to HERMIES.

12. No 29896 Pte Dunn R. Brown awarded 10 days F.P. No 2 & forfeits
Award by   2 days pay under Royal Warrant; 10.12.18 for - Breaking
C.O.   out of Billets after "Last Post" remaining absent until 09.35 hrs
           10.12.18 (12 hrs 10 minutes)

13. Corporal C. Maxted "C" Coy has been allotted new Regt No
Regimental viz No 203676 of G/9047/7.
Number

14. [illegible]
Leave

[illegible lines]

True copy J. Shipton C/Lt
                          (Sgd) J.E. Shipton
ADJT 1/11   2/Lt Hillman Rgt.   3rd The Queens Regt
FILE 1/2
War Diary 13/14

SECRET   Battalion Orders No 256   Copy No 13
              by Major P.B. Avery. M.C.
              Comdg. 1st The Queen's Reg.

                                              December 11th 1918

Detail for tomorrow
Subaltern of the day   2/Lieut J.H. TINDALL

Ref Map: VALENCIENNES 1/100.000

1. The Battalion will parade ready to move off at 08.50hrs and will march in order H.Q, B, C, Drums, D.A. Transport, to HERMIES distance approx. 8 miles.

2. Cookers will march with the Regimental Transport.

3. Starting point — where light Railway crosses road 650x due S of Y in RUMILLY. H.Q will pass this point at 09.00 hrs

4. ROUTE — MARCOING — RIBECOURT — HAVRINCOURT.

5. Capt K.M. EAST is detailed as billeting officer. The normal billeting party will parade under him with bicycles at the Guard Room at 07.30hrs tomorrow and will proceed to HERMIES reporting to Staff Captain at O./c Staging Camps Office, HERMIES at 08.30hrs.

6. B" Signalling officer will arrange Synchronisation of watches at 08.20 hrs

7. Blankets will be stacked where they were issued today by 07.00 hrs. Officers Valises will be at Q.M. Stores by 07.45 hrs Mess Baskets will be at H.Q Mess by 08.10hrs.

8. Distances as laid down will be maintained throughout.

9. The following points noticed by G.O.C Division today are published for compliance:
   (a) Neck chains were not worn in all cases. The Corps have ordered that these will be invariably be worn and this order will be strictly observed.
   (b) If the O.C Company elects to walk he will detail another officer to ride.
   (c) More attention must be paid to the maintenance of distances on the march.
   (d) The method of carrying waterproof sheet on pack was not uniform. O.C. Coys will ensure that the standard method is observed.

10. Under authority delegated by H.M. The King, the Army
AWARDS Commander has awarded the under mentioned decorations to the following:
                Authority 3rd Army R.O. 1891 d/3rd Dec.
        Bar to M.C. — Capt G.H. Cordelet. M.C
        M.C.   — Capt W.A. North.
        D.C.M.   — No 039 Sergt D.H. Ayley
                      Scots
        The congratulations of the Army, Div & Bde Commanders coupled with those of the C.O. are to be conveyed to the recipients.

11. ELECTION. In most cases where doubt exists regarding the politics of candidates for the forthcoming election, newspapers showing these particulars will be issued shortly to enable voters to record their votes. O.C Companies will impress upon all ranks of their Company that although it is the duty of all voters as citizens to exercise the franchise, although there is no compulsion in this respect

                                              continued

Battalion Orders No 256.   page 2.

12. XMAS MAIL It is notified for information that the following dates are those on which letters and parcels intended for delivery in the British Isles by Xmas should be posted

	Letters	Parcels
British Isles (except London)	18th	16th
London	19th	17th

13. Appointments Lieut (a/Capt) R. H. Maddock. M.C. is appointed to the command of "D" Coy from 10th Dec.

Lieut (a/Capt) W. A. North, M.C. is appointed a/Capt (additional) on ceasing to command "D" Coy, from 10 Dec.

14. The Battalion will move on 13th inst to FAVREUIL.

Copies:
```
C.O.        No 1
Coys        No 2/5
T.O.        . 6
Q.M.        . 7
R.S.M.      . 8
B.S.O.      . 9
HQ.MESS     .10
ADJT        .11
FILE        .12
WAR.DIARY   13/14
```

(Sgd) J. E. Shipton
Lieut & Adjt
Bn The Queens Regt

True copy
J Shipton Lt
a/Adjt 1st Bn The Queen's Regt

SECRET   Battalion Orders No: 254
          by Major H.B. Avery MC   COPY. No:
          Comdg. Bn. The Queen's Regt.
                                        December 13th 1918

Detail for tomorrow
   Subaltern of the day.   2/Lieut R.F.K. ROBERTS.

Ref. Maps LENS & VALENCIENNES 1/100,000

1. The Battalion will parade ready to move off at 0915
hrs, head of Column will rest on outskirts of village
and will march to FAVREUIL, in order HQ. C.D. Drums
A.B. Regimental Transport. Distance approx: 11 miles.

2. O.C. "B" Company will detail 1 NCO and 6 men to act
as the Stragglers Party. They will march in rear
of the Battalion and will collect all stragglers if
side able to march and bring them along in a
party. NCO i/c will report at O.Room. FAVREUIL on
arrival.

3. Starting Point. - Road Junction 300 yds due S. of
N. in DOIGNIES. H.Q. will pass this point at 0937 hrs.
Route :- DOIGNIES - BEAUMETZ - LES - CAMBRAI - VELU -
LEBUCQUIERE - FREMICOURT - BEAUGNATRE.

4. There will be a halt from 1150 hrs to 1300 hrs for dinners
Cookers will therefore march in rear of their respective
Companies.

5. Lieut D.V. BERNARD is detailed as Billeting Officer
The normal billeting party will parade with bicycles
under him on road in front of H.Q tents at
0715 hrs. Party will proceed to FAVREUIL, reporting
to Staff Captain at O.K. Staging Camps Office at
0830 hrs.

6. Distances as laid down will be maintained.

7. Batta S.O. will arrange for synchronisation of
watches at 0840 hrs.

8. Blankets will be rolled by 0700 hrs and left in
tents until orders are given for loading.
Officers Valises will be put on Baggage Wagon at
0815 hrs.

9. On 14th inst the Battalion will march to W. of ALBERT.

10. O's C Coys will render a return to O.Room by 1800 hrs
tomorrow showing total No of rounds S.A.A. carried
on the men in their Coy.

Officers.
C.O. No 1.   Coy 2-5.
2/ Lieut   6+7 RSM 8.
R.S.O.   9. Names 10
Adjt   11   File 12
War Diary 13+14.

SECRET   Battalion Orders No: 258   Copy No
                by Major N.B. AVERY. MC
                Comdg:- 1st The Queens Regt
                                              Friday Decr 13th 1918.

Detail for tomorrow
Subaltern of the day   2/Lieut H Y SAVAGE.

Ref. Map. LENS 1/100,000

1. The Battalion will parade ready to move off in order:- HQ. D. A. Drums. B. C. at 0825 hrs and will march to 10 of ALBERT, distance approx 15 miles.

2. Starting Point:- Cross Roads 450 yds W. of F in FAVREUIL. Battn Hd Qrs will pass this point at 0900 hrs.

3. Route: - BAPAUME - ALBERT.

4. There will be a halt for dinners from 11.50 hrs to 13.00 hrs. Cookers will therefore accompany their respective Companies.

5. The normal distances will be maintained throughout the march.

6. Lt. F.J.F MOULTRIE is detailed as billeting Officer. The normal billeting party will parade with bicycles under him at the northern end of Camp at 0730 hrs. Party will proceed to O i/c Staging Camp Office W of ALBERT reporting to Staff Captain at 0900 hrs.

7. Battn Signalling Officer will arrange for the synchronisation of watches by 0800 hrs.

8. Blankets will be rolled and handed in at QM Stores by 0700 hrs.
   Officers Valises will be loaded on Baggage Wagons by 0730 hrs.
   Mess Baskets will be loaded on Mess Cart by 0745 hrs.
   Sick Parade 0645 hrs.   Reveille 06 15 hrs.
   Breakfasts 0700 hrs.

9. On the 15th Inst the Battalion will march to PONT NOYELLES - QUERRIEU - BUSSY AREA.

                        (Sgd) J G Shipton Lieut & Adjt.
                                1st Bn The Queens Regt
True copy

      J G Shipton Lt
      1st Bn The Queens Rgt

Copies No:
C.O. No: 1
Coys. No: 2-5
T.O. & Q.M. 6-7
R.S.M. 8
B/S.O. 9
H.Q. Mess 10
Adjt. 11
FILE. 12 War Diary 13/14.

SECRET.   Battalion Orders No 259   Copy No 14
                       by Major N. BAVERY. M.C
                       Comdg: Batn The Queen's Regt   Saturday Dec 14th 1918

Detail for tomorrow
    Subaltern of the day   Lieut G.A. IONIDES

Ref Maps LENS & AMIENS 1/100,000.

1. The Battn will parade ready to move off at 09.00 hrs tomorrow and will march in order HQ, A, B, Drums, C, D, Regtl Transport, to QUERRIEU area, distance approx: 10 miles.

2. Starting point: Junction of ALBERT-AMIENS and ALBERT-DERNANCOURT roads. Bn HQ will pass this point at 09.13 hrs.
   Route: LAHOUSSOYE.

3. There will be a halt from 11.50 hrs to 13.00 hrs for dinners. Cookers will therefore march in rear of their respective Companies.

4. Capt K.M. EAST is detailed as billeting officer. The normal billeting party with 1 BHQ runner in addition will parade under him with bicycles at Southern end of Camp at 07.15 hrs.

5. Distances as laid down will be maintained throughout.

6. Battn Signalling Officer will arrange for synchronisation of watches by 08.30 hrs.

7. Blankets will be rolled and stacked where they were drawn today by 07.00 hrs.
   Officers Valises will be loaded on Baggage wagon by 08.00 hrs
   Mess Kits will be loaded on Mess Cart by 08.15 hrs.
            Reveille will be 06.30 hrs
            Breakfasts   " " 07.15 hrs

8. On 16th inst the Battn will march to ARGOEUVRES area.

9. The personnel of the Regtl Transport will not wear greatcoats or warm coats on the line of march unless such dress is ordered in Battalion Orders.

10. It has come to the notice of the C.O. that men are in the habit of coming on parade with very dirty puttees and boots. Although conditions are against the usual cleanliness expected in this Battalion, O.C. Companies will take steps to see that attempts are made, 10 minutes with a knife before parade will make a great difference.

11. One Officer & 10 Other Ranks 17th Div will join the Battalion for this march & be attached to "A" Company

Copies:-
C.O.   No 1
Coys   2/5
TO & QM 6/7
R.S.M.   8
D.S.O.   9
HQ MESS 10
ADJT   11
FILE   12
WAR DIARY 13/14

(sgd) F.E. Shipton
                        Lieut o/a A/
                Batn The Queens Regt

True copy
F. Shipton Lt/
for Batn The Queens Regt

SECRET Battalion Orders No 260   Copy No 13
by Major N. B. Avery M.C
Comdg: Bn The Queens Regt

Detail for tomorrow   Sunday
  Subaltern of the day   2/Lieut A.J. GREENAWAY
Ref Map AMIENS 1/100.000

1. The Battalion will parade ready to move off at 0855 hrs and will march in order H.Q. "D" "C" Drums "B" "A" to BREILLY distance approx 11 miles. Cookers will march in rear of respective Companies. There will be a halt from 11.50 hrs to 13.00 hrs for dinners. O.C. "A" Company will detail 1 N.C.O (effective) and three men to act as stragglers party. These will march in rear of Company.

2. The normal distances will be maintained throughout the march.

3. Starting point and route will be notified later.

4. Lieut O.V. Bernard is detailed as billeting Officer. The normal billeting party will parade under him with bicycles at O Room at 07.30 hrs. The party will report to Town Major BREILLY.

5. 2/Lieut A.J. SHERLOCK is detailed to ascertain from the MAIRES if the inhabitants are preferring any claims against the Battn and will settle them. If necessary he will make his own way to BREILLY.

6. Blankets will be rolled & stacked at Q.M. Stores by 07.00 hrs. Officers Valises will be loaded on baggage wagons by 08.00 hrs. In future all valises must be more tidily rolled. Mess Baskets will be at H.Q. Mess by 08.15 hrs.

7. The Bn Signalling Officer will arrange for synchronisation of watches by 08.30 hrs.

8. The undermentioned proceed on leave to U.K. tomorrow by train leaving AMIENS at 12.00 hrs. They will parade at O Room at 08.30 hrs fully equipped & carry the days ration. They will be paid prior to departure & A.B. 64 will have period of leave inserted. The party will parade sick tomorrow at sick parade.
No 203210 Pte Paine R. "A" Coy No 10240 Pte Webb A "A" Coy No 5930 Pte Groves W "A" Coy No 11084 Pte Bates W "B" Coy No 10620 Pte Meme ? "C" Coy No 3736 Pte Wilkie C "C" Coy No 25052 Pte Binley C "C" Coy No 63389 Pte Pyett W "D" Coy No 4659 Sergt Pullen H. "D" Coy No... Pte Burgess A "D" Coy No 63261 ... period of leave 17. 31.12.18
No 8963 Sgt Winder W granted leave to U.K. 17.12.18 – 17.1.19.

9. On 15th inst the Battn will march to final destination.

10. The party of 1 Off & 10 O.R. 14th Div will proceed to their destination under orders issued separately to O i/c

Copies
H.Q No 1
Coys 2/5
TO:QM 6/7
R.S.M 8
E.S.O 9
QM MESS 10
ADJT 11
FILE 12
WAR DIARY 13/14

True copy   J. Shipton
J. Shipton 2/Lt
1st Bn The Queens Regt

SECRET   Copy No 13
          Battalion Orders No 261
          by Major. H. B. Avery. M.C
          Comdg. Battn The Queens Regt

Detail for tomorrow   Monday, Decr 16th 1918
Subaltern of the day   2/Lieut F. S. F. MOULTRIE
Ref Maps:- AMIENS & DIEPPE 1/100,000

1. The Battalion will parade ready to move off in order
   H.Q. "C" "D" Drums "A" "B" Regtl Transport at 08.55 hrs. Head
   of column will rest on Q.M. Stores.
   The Battalion will march to CAMPS & HALLIVILLERS
   There will be a halt for dinners from 11.50 hrs to 13 hrs
   Cookers will therefore be in rear of their respective companies

2. Starting Point:- Road junction ½ mile W.S.W. of "B" in
   BREILLY. Battalion Head Quarters will pass this Point
   at 09.00 hrs

3. Route:- POURDRINOY - MOLLIENS VIDAME.

4. The usual distances will be maintained throughout
   the march.

5. Battn Signalling Officer will arrange for synchronisation
   of watches by 08.30 hrs.

6. Lieut D. V. Bernard is detailed to ascertain from the
   MAIRE if there are any claims outstanding and if
   admissable will settle them. He will if necessary
   make his own way to new area.

7. Blankets will be stacked as under
   "A" & "B" Companies under Archway by Guard and
   "C" "D" & HQrs in Q.M. Stores by 08.00 hrs.
   Valises will be loaded on baggage wagon by 08.00 hrs
   Mess Baskets will be at H.Q. Mess by 08.15 hrs.

8. All bicycles at present on charge of Companies
   will be returned to H.Q. Signals by 08.00 hrs.

9. On arrival in new area O.C. Companies will
   ensure that Battalion Standing Orders re FIRES are
   complied with, without delay.

Copies:-
C.O. No 1
Coys . 2/5
T.O. & Q.M. 6/7
RSM . 8
B.S.O. . 9   True Copy   Sgd J. E. Sheldon
HQ Mess . 10   "Lieut & Adjt"
Adjt . 11   J. Shipton /Lt   1st Bn "The Queens Regt"
File . 12
WAR DIARY 13/14   1st Bn Queens Regt

Army Form C. 2118.

WAR DIARY
or
INTELLIGENCE SUMMARY.
(Erase heading not required.)

33 1/R.W. Surrey Bn. 7th June 1917

Place	Date	Hour	Summary of Events and Information	Remarks and references to Appendices
CAMP				APP. I
			1. Paraded as previously arranged for the distribution of Medal Ribands by Lt Col Reginald Turner, K.C.B. The Transport was drawn up in column of route on main ARRAS–BETHUNE ROAD attached to the wagons. The C.O. handed ribands to officers of the various platoons &c. He expressed his approval of the Rifle Transport. After parade the turn out of the Battn. field kitchen followed by 3 gratis E.Y.	
			2. Warning order for move to KHAYRE received. Preparations for move commenced. L.G. classes continued instruction. En ordres for move issued.	B.O. 275
			3. The Bn. paraded at 0955 hrs and marched to entrainment at the station. Men dined (Gave Macuitano) before entraining for HAVRE. Train attained at HAVRE at about 0500 hrs. It was found that 1 Major G.S. & 1 man of Lewis Gr. were missing. After obtaining the necessary kit Bn. marched to No. 2 Rest Camp where it was accommodated.	36 1/R.W.S.
4.				

1/ Queens go to
98th My Bde

33   1/R.W. Surrey R.
     TRIPOLI 1917
     War Diary for July and Aug

Army Form C. 2118.

WAR DIARY
or
INTELLIGENCE SUMMARY.
(Erase heading not required.)

Place	Date	Hour	Summary of Events and Information	Remarks and references to Appendices
CAMPS	1		The Battalion paraded as strong as possible on 30 yds frontage for the distribution of Medal Ribands by Major General Sir Reginald Pinney, K.C.B. The Transport was drawn up in column front or main ARRAINGEMENT on ARRAINGED POYX attack. They had moved inside to the wajed. The got marched ribands. He expressed his approval of the smartness & steadiness of the turn-out of the Rgtl. Transport. The parade then played the to an association football match, Battalion by 3 goals to 1.	APP 1.
	2		Warning order for move ETHAVRE received. Preparation for move commenced. L.G. classes continued instruction. Bn orders for move issued.	B.O. 275
	3		The Bn. paraded at 0955 hrs and marched to the station. After dinner the Battalion for HAVRE (under Major G.C. Gaw Maidens) at about 0500 hrs.	
	4		The Bn. detrained at HAVRE & marched (under G.T.) were to 1½ hrs from station that Major G.S. was marched. It was found Afte detraining Bn. marched to rest camp ills Bn. marched to marching. After detraining it was accommodated. Coy 8. No Rest Camp	36 1/RWS

WAR DIARY
or
INTELLIGENCE SUMMARY. 1st Bn Mulhuenis Regt

Army Form C. 2118.
PAGE 2

Place	Date	Hour	Summary of Events and Information	Remarks and references to Appendices
HAVRE	5		Cleaning up Camp. Impressed at 10.45hrs for Divine Service at which was held an Salvation Army Hut. Hut O. Inspection group after disperse.	
-"-	6		Bn Impressed at 09.40 hrs for route march. Route Canal Bank - Harfleur - GRAVILLE.	
-"-	7		Company Officers routine carried out. L.G. classes continued instruction.	
-"-	8		Training & General Routine.	
-"-	9		Training & General Routine.	
-"-	10		Training & General Routine.	
-"-	11		Training & General Routine. Capt & Adjt R. NEVINS. M.C. reported on recovering from wounds and resumed duties of Adjutant.	
-"-	12		Battalion attended Divine Service in Camp.	

WAR DIARY or INTELLIGENCE SUMMARY

Army Form C. 2118.

JANUARY 1919   1st Batt. "THE QUEEN'S"   Page 3

Place	Date	Hour	Summary of Events and Information	Remarks and references to Appendices
HAVRE	1/13		Battalion paraded at 10.00 hrs and marched to Camp No 17 HARFLEUR where quarters were allotted. Move ordered in consequence of Scheme for the forming of No 2 DIRTY Camp on ground now covered by Nos 17, 18 and 19 Camps. The personnel for which is to be detailed by the Battalion. No 1 DIRTY Camp at SANVIC already visited by receiving men for dispersal on demobilization was visited by officers during the past week to gain knowledge of the working.	
No 17 Camp HARFLEUR	14		Training and general routine — looking parties to assist R.E. at hut building — Strength 90 O.R. were found &c.	
"	15 6 18		ditto	
"	/19		Battalion attended Divine Service.	
"	20 &25		Battalion employed throughout the week in preparing No 2. Reception Camp — for men for Demobilization.	

WAR DIARY
or
INTELLIGENCE SUMMARY.
(Erase heading not required.)

Army Form C. 2118.

1st Bath "The Queen's" Regt

JANUARY 1919

Place	Date	Hour	Summary of Events and Information	Remarks and references to Appendices
HARWICH 1st2 sheppy 1/31st Camp	26		Whole Battalion employed in the working of No 2. Reception Camp (Constitution) which has taken the place of Camps 17.18. and 19 Numbers sent fit depart to date:— Officers Lieut W.A. IONIDES. Regt. Queens BULL. F.E. SPROSTON. H.Y. SAVAGE. Other ranks — 161.	
	1st February 1919.			

B Russel Lieut Colonel
Comdg. 1st Batth "The Queen's" Regt.

Appx 1

LIST OF OFFICERS AND OTHER RANKS WHO WERE PRESENTED WITH
MEDAL RIBANDS BY DIVISIONAL COMMANDER
ON 1st JANUARY 1919.
****

Bar to Military Cross	-	Capt. G.F.ASHPITEL M.C.
Military Cross	-	" W.A.NORTH M.C.
" "	-	2/Lieut. S.M. HOWCROFT M.C.
" "	-	" H.C.CRAWLEY M.C.
" "	-	" J.RUDKIN M.C.
" "	-	" C.S.CLARK M.C.
Bar to Military Medal	-	39833 Pte. J. FEARN M.M.
Military Medal	-	78876 Sgt. C.BURGESS M.M.
" "	-	206024 Cpl. G. JOHNSON M.M.
" "	-	78881 " A. HOWELL M.M.
" "	-	25238 " W. PULLEN M.M.
" "	-	23684 L/Cpl E.BAKER M.M.
" "	-	25171 " A.WHITTLE M.M.
" "	-	202654 Pte A.WORLAND M.M.
" "	-	30261 " W.CLAPP M.M.
" "	-	23695 " J.E.PARRY M.M.
" "	-	6795 " S.SMITH M.M.
Merritorious Service Medal	-	5873 Sgt/Drmr. J.WINTER.

****

SECRET   Battalion Orders No 245   Copy No 13
by Lieut Col R Bellamy D.S.O.
Comdg: 1st Bn The Queens Regt

Detail for tomorrow   January 2nd 1919
Subaltern of the day   Lieut A.E. Saunders

Ref Map DIEPPE 1/100.000

1. The Battalion will move to HAVRE tomorrow 3rd by march route to POIX and by train to final destination.

2. The Transport will march in advance of the Battalion, passing X Roads at S end of CAMPS village at 08.45 hrs. Vehicles from HALLEVILLERS will join column at this point. O.C. "C" & "D" Coys will ensure that the vehicles on their charge are ready loaded at 08.15 hr. Coy chargers will proceed with the Regt Transport.

3. The Battalion less C & D Coys will parade in order H.Q. "A" "B" ready to move off at 10.00 hrs. Head of column will rest on X Roads at S end of CAMPS.
The Battalion will march to POIX via LINCHEUX & THIEULLOY. Starting point:- Road Junction 200x W of Ly in LINCHEUX. Column will pass this point at 10.30 hrs. C & D Companies will join column at this point. Order of march from starting point H.Q. A.B.C.D.
Usual distance will be maintained throughout.

4. An advance party consisting of Capt K.M.EAST, the R.Q.M.S and 1 N.C.O. per Company & Bn H.Q. & 1 Signaller Bn H.Q. will rendezvous with bicycles at X roads at S end of CAMPS at 08.30 hrs. N.C.O's C & D Coys will use cycles at present on charge of B's & Coys. Remainder will arrange to draw from Signallers.

5. O.C. Coys will ensure that all waterbottles are filled with drinking water prior to moving off.

6. O.C. Coys will be responsible that all latrines & refuse pits are filled in and that their Company areas are left in a clean & sanitary condition.

7. The baggage waggon will call for valises at C & D Coys at 07.30 hrs. Valises of H.Q, A & B Coys will be at C.B.Stores by 08.00 hrs.

8. Blankets rolled in tens the short way of the blanket, securely tied & clearly labelled will be ready for loading by lorries tomorrow as under, by 08.00 hrs.
A.B.C & D Coys at respective H.Q.
Bn H.Q. at Q.M Stores.
O.C. "D" Coy will detail 1 N.C.O. to take charge of C & D Coys blanket lorry.

9. Mess Baskets will be ready for loading as under at respective H.Q.
C & D Coys   07.15 hrs   A.B & H.Q. 07.45 hrs
(continued)

Battalion Orders No. 2/5 page 2.

10. All spare boxes will be at Q.M. Stores by 07.30 hrs
11. O.C "A" Coy will detail 1 N.C.O. + 5 men as ration fatigue, they will report to the Transport Officer & march with the Reg. Transport.
12. The following points re journey will be communicated to all ranks.
    (a) No water will be drunk or water bottles filled from any source not reported fit by the R.T.O.
    (b) All doors of covered trucks & carriages on right hand side of train will be kept closed.
    (c) Brake vans are reserved for Railway staff and are not to be used by troops.
13. Rations will be issued as under:-
    (a) Breakfast in billets.
    (b) Dinners at POIX
    (c) remainder of rations for 3rd carried on man
    (d) For consumption 4th on arrival at HAVRE.
14. The Colours will be carried by Lieut S.M. HOWCROFT, M.C. and 2/Lieut F.R.F. MOULTRIE. Coverers will be detailed from B.H.Q.. party will parade at H.Q Mess at 07.45 hrs & march in rear of B.Coy. The packs of this party will be carried on blanket lorry.
15. Sick parade will be at 07.15 hrs for HALLEVILLERS and 07.45 hrs at CAMPS.
16. The undermentioned will proceed on leave to U.K. tomorrow 3rd period of leave 5/19.1.19.
    "A" Coy.
    No. 21678 L/Cpl C. Jennings No. 39833 Pte J. Hearn No. 25823 Pte F. Batchelor No. 202691 Pte F. Mussell.
    C. Coy
    No. 41595 Pte O. Geer.
    The above will be paid & period of leave inserted in AB64 prior to departure. They will parade at O. Room for Medical inspection at 07.30 hrs & fully equipped, ready to proceed at 09.00hrs.

Copies
C.O.   No. 1
Coys.   2/5
T.O.   6
Q.M.   7
R.S.M. 8
B.S.D. 9
H.Q Mess 10
ADJT   11
FILE   12
War Diary 13/14

sgd J.R. Shipton
Lieut Adjt
1st Bn The Queen's

WAR DIARY 1st Batt. "THE QUEEN'S" Army Form C. 2118.

or

INTELLIGENCE SUMMARY. FEBRUARY 1919

(Erase heading not required.)

Vol 5 37 1/R.W.S.

Place	Date	Hour	Summary of Events and Information	Remarks and references to Appendices
HARFLEUR	1st		Whole Battalion employed in the working of N°2 Reception Camp – 1 Sgt 9 men sent for dispersal	
"	2nd		Ditto — 4 Jm. Officers Divine Service – 1 Cpl 1 man " " "	
"	3rd		Whole Battalion employed on the working of N°2 Reception Camp – 12 O.R. lists under A.D.1 v. 7. 10. 12. 18. finally approved – attestations completed – sent to 2.A.G. 3. Ech.	
"	4th		Ditto — 1 Sgt 9 men sent for dispersal	
"	5th		Work as on 3rd — 7 men sent for dispersal – 1 man enlisted under A.D. 1 v. 7. 10. 12. 18. finally approved – attestations completed sent to 2.A.G. 3. Ech.	
"	6		Work as on 3rd — 1 Cpl 2 men sent for dispersal.	
"	7		Work as on 3rd — 2 men sent for dispersal. 1 Sgt 1 Cpl 4 men dispersed from short leave in England.	
"	8		Work as on 3rd — 2 men sent for dispersal. 9 men dispersed from short leave in England.	

Army Form C. 2118.
Page 2

WAR DIARY
INTELLIGENCE SUMMARY.

1st Batln "THE QUEEN'S" FEBRUARY 1919

Place	Date	Hour	Summary of Events and Information	Remarks and references to Appendices
HARFLEUR	9th		Bn & Battalion employed in working No 2 Reception Camp — Those available attend Divine Service	
"	10th		— Ditto —	
"	11th		— Ditto — 1 Sgt. 2 L/Sgt. 21 men sent for Dispersal	
"	12		— Ditto — 1 Man sent for Dispersal	
"	13		— Ditto — 1 Cpl. 9 men sent for Dispersal	
"	14		— Ditto — 1 Sgt 6 men sent for dispersal 2nd Lieut BATTSON A.C. to ROUEN for Front Service	
"	15		— Ditto — 1/Lt A. PINKIE 1 Cpl 9 men sent for dispersal	
"	16		— Ditto — Divine Service — Voluntary. 1 Sgt Reuwin sent for Dispersal. Lieut SM MOWCROFT M.C. also sent for Dispersal	

WAR DIARY

INTELLIGENCE SUMMARY. 1st Batn. THE QUEEN'S Regt.

FEBRUARY 1919   Army Form C. 2118.
Page 3

Place	Date	Hour	Summary of Events and Information	Remarks and references to Appendices
HARFLEUR	17		Whole Battalion employed on the working of No 3 Kineton Camp	
"	18		— Ditto —	1 Man sent for dispersal.
"	19		— Ditto — Capt E.A.G. POWELL-JONES M.C. Capt P.A. WATTS. Lieutenant J.C. WHITING. 2/Lieuts R.E. WOODS. J.R. SPEEDING W.H. MERCER. C.G. LOVE F. RAWLINSON. P.E. TOWNSON M.C. J.W. NORTHWOOD and 24 Other ranks joined from 6th Battn. 1 Sergt 2 men sent for dispersal.	
"	20		Whole Battalion employed on working of No 2 Kineton Camp. Capt G.F. ASHPITEL M.C. and 7 men sent for dispersal	
"	21		— Ditto —	Two men sent for dispersal.
"	22		— Ditto —	
"	23		— Ditto —	Divine Service voluntary. 1 C/Sm. & 6 men sent for dispersal

WAR DIARY
INTELLIGENCE SUMMARY of 1st Bn. THE QUEEN'S Regt.

FEBRUARY 1919   Army Form C. 2118.
Page 4.

Place	Date	Hour	Summary of Events and Information	Remarks and references to Appendices
HARFLEUR	24		Whole Battalion employed on unloading of Reception Camp. 2 Sgts. 2 Cpls. 9 men sent for dispersal	
"	25		Ditto. 6 men sent for dispersal.	
"	26		Ditto — Cadre 2nd Batt. passed through from Italy en-route for England — 3 men sent for dispersal	
"	27		Ditto — 2 Sgts. 4 Cpls 11 men sent for dispersal	
"	28		Ditto — Lieut W.E. LAWRENCE, M.C., H.E. EPPS, 180 O.Rs rank of Pte. East Kent Regt (The Buffs) joined Battalion under G.H.Q. instructions and taken on strength. 2 men sent for dispersal. Field H. BASSETT to dispersal station from Leave 26 ins.	

R.C. Windle
Lieut Colonel
Comdg. The Queen's Regt.

WAR DIARY
INTELLIGENCE SUMMARY

1st Batt. "THE QUEEN'S" Regiment
Army Form C. 2118.
Page 1.

MARCH 1919

Place	Date	Hour	Summary of Events and Information	Remarks and references to Appendices
No 2 Reception Camp	1st		Whole Battalion employed on working of Camp — 4 men sent for dispersal	N.V. 5.3
HARFLEUR	2nd		" Voluntary Arms Range — 1 Officer —	
"	3		" 1 Man sent for dispersal	
"	4		" 1 Corpl sent for dispersal	
"	5		" All available attended Short Route March	
"	6		" 1 Sergt. 5 men sent for dispersal	
"	7		" 1 man sent for dispersal	
"	8		" 1 man sent for dispersal — A.P.C. TULLEY H.Q. O.R. 2nd Lieut. R.H. WRIGHT joined from 10th E. Kent Regt "The Buffs" and E.H.Q. in Future.	

38 1/R.W

WAR DIARY 1st Batt "THE QUEEN'S" Regt

INTELLIGENCE SUMMARY

Army Form C. 2118.
Page 2

Place	Date	Hour	Summary of Events and Information	Remarks and references to Appendices
No 2 Reception Camp	9		Whole Battalion employed in working of Camp – Voluntary Divine Service –	
HARFLEUR	10		5 men sent for Disposal	
"	11		1 Serjt sent for Disposal	
"	12		3 men sent for Disposal G.O.C. Bse inspected and addressed Draft 170 E Kent	
"	13		2 men sent for Disposal 1st Bn Middlesex Regt commenced to taking over of No 2 Reception Camp – 1 Capt 3 men sent for Disposal	A.Bs 62.
"	14		A"and "C" Coys paraded at 2pm and marched to SANVIC for duty at No 7. Disposal Camp. 2 Sgts 12 men sent for Disposal	
"	15		Relief by 1st Bn Middlesex Regt completed. "D" Coy on relief overseas Duties in No 11 Camp. Bn H.Qrs D-13 Camp. 2 Sgts 2 Cpls 7 men sent for Disposal	

WAR DIARY
INTELLIGENCE SUMMARY

(Erase heading not required.)

2nd Bn "THE QUEEN'S" Regt

Army Form C. 2118.

March 1919

Page 3

Place	Date	Hour	Summary of Events and Information	Remarks and references to Appendices
HARFLEUR	16		Battalion returned by E.F.C. from the Details Bn attached Parade Service 10:30am	
"	17		D Coy moved to CINDER CITY and B Coy to BELGIAN Compound for duty under respective Commandants. 4 Cpls 10 men sent for dispersal	
"	18		2 men sent for dispersal	
"	19		1 man sent for dispersal	
"	20		1 Sergt 6 men sent for dispersal	
"	21		Lieut E.R. TEDSTONE - 2 Sergts 8 men sent for dispersal. Lt Col R.J BELLAMY D.S.O. Royal Sussex Regt in accordance with instructions from G.H.Q. proceeds to join 30th Division. Major N.B. AVERY M.C. assumed command of the Battalion. 2nd Lieut 1 W.O. 1 Sergt 1 Cpl 35 O.R. joined from England.	

WAR DIARY
INTELLIGENCE SUMMARY. 1st Batt. "THE QUEEN'S" Regt

Army Form C. 2118.

March 1919

Page 4

(Erase heading not required.)

Place	Date	Hour	Summary of Events and Information	Remarks and references to Appendices
HARFLEUR	21st		Farewell message to Battalion by Lt Col R. Bellamy D.S.O on leaving our Command	
			"It is with much regret that I am leaving the 1st "Queen's" to Command another Battalion — I have felt it a great honour to Command the Battalion though for what a period and wish to thank all Officers W.O's N.C.O's men for the good work they have done when in No 2 Buxton Camp. The discipline has been excellent also and I hope it will not be long before I have the pleasure of serving with the Battalion again."	
"	22nd		Cpl Queen sent for trepaned	
"	23		Battalion attended Divine service after which the band played to the public	
"	24th		Lieut Col CLARKE M.C. sent for disposal	

WAR DIARY
INTELLIGENCE SUMMARY.
(Erase heading not required.)

of 1st Bn "THE QUEEN'S" Regt
Page 5

Army Form C. 2118.
March 1919

Place	Date	Hour	Summary of Events and Information	Remarks and references to Appendices
HARFLEUR	25		8 men sent for dispersal.	
"	26			
"	27		Lieut W.H. MERCER and 2 men sent for dispersal.	
"	28		1 Sgt 6 men sent for dispersal.	
"	29		10 men sent for dispersal	
"	30		Battalion attended Divine Service. Lieut J.R. SPEEDING sent for dispersal.	
"	31		C.S.M. W. PHILIP sent for dispersal.	

31st March 1919

W.B. Avent, Major
Comdg 1st Bn "The Queen's" Regt

No. 12
War Diary

BATTALION ROUTINE ORDER NO. 62,
by
Lieut-Colonel R. SELLAR D.S.O.,
Comdg: 1st Battalion "THE QUEEN'S" Regiment.
Thursday, 13th March 1919.

1. The Battalion will be relieved by the 1st Battalion THE MIDDLESEX Regiment on 13th March 1919 and following days.

2. "A" and "B" Companies, 1st Battn: THE MIDDLESEX Regiment arrived this day to take over Delouser relieving "A" Coy. Relief will be complete by 06.00 hrs. on the 14th instant.

3. Nos. 1, 2, and 3 Wings will be relieved as follows:-

   14th inst - "B" Coy. 1st MIDDLESEX Regt. relieves Nos. 2 and 3 Wings. i.e. hrs. "C" & "D" Coys. by 12.00
   15th " - "C" Coy.   do.   relieves No. 1 Wing i.e. "B" Coy. by 12.00 hrs.

   Battalion Headquarters will be relieved by 12.00 hrs. on 15th inst., when Command of Camp passes to Officer Commanding, 1st Battn: MIDDLESEX Regt.

4. After completion of relief, the Battalion will be disposed as follows:
   Battalion Headquarters and Q.M. Stores - No. 13 Camp.
   Move will take place on morning of 15th instant.
   "A" and "C" Coys. - No. 1 Dispatch Camp, relieving 1 Coy. ARGYLL & SUTHERLAND HIGHLANDERS, and will furnish the personnel for running the Camp under the orders of the Camp Commandant. Move to take place after dinners on the 14th. inst. under orders to be issued by Capt. R.H. PHILPOT M.C. (copy to be forwarded to the Adjutant). Advance party to move by lorry at 08.30 vide instructions already issued to Officers Commanding "A" and "C" Coys. and Quartermaster.
   "B" Coy. remain in present billets. Officers to be accommodated in Quarters in No. 16 CAMP as arranged with 1st MIDDLESEX Regt.
   "D" Coy. to No. 14 CAMP. To move under orders of Coy. Commander on morning of the 15th instant.

5. Transport for blankets etc. will be arranged by Quartermaster.

6. No barrack furniture is to be removed from present quarters.

7. O.C. Coys. will take such steps as will ensure that huts, tents, Officers' Quarters, and ground in their area are left clean. They will inspect same and report to the Adjutant prior to moving off.

8. Completion of all moves and relief will be reported at once to Battalion Headquarters.

9. Acknowledge.

(Sgd) R. NEVINS, Capt. & Adjt.,
1st Battn: "THE QUEEN'S" Regt.

Copies issued as under at 15.45 hrs.

1. C.O.   2. No. 1 Coy.   3. No. 2 Coy.
4. No. 3 Coy. 5. No. 4 Coy.   6. Q.M.
7. R.S.M.   8. MIDDLESEX.   9. Adjutant.
10. File.   11 & 12 War Diary. 13 & 14 Spare.

WAR DIARY
INTELLIGENCE SUMMARY.
(Erase heading not required.)

1st Bttn "THE QUEEN'S" Army Form C. 2118.
APRIL 1919   Page 1.

Place	Date	Hour	Summary of Events and Information	Remarks and references to Appendices
HARFLEUR	1st		General Routine – A.W. BERNARD – 2 Sgt 1 Cpl 4 men sent for dispersal	
"	2nd		General Routine – 1 man sent for dispersal	
"	3rd		General Routine – Lieut (a/Capt) W.A. NORTH M.C. 1 Sgt 2 men sent for dispersal R.E. WOODS.	
"	4th		General Routine – Lieut A.J. GREENAWAY – 1 man sent for dispersal	
"	5th		General Routine –	
"	6th		General Routine – Cogo attended Divine Service.	
"	7th		General Routine	
"	8th		General Routine 2 men sent for dispersal.	

Army Form C. 2118.

1st Bn. "The Queen's"

Page 2

WAR DIARY
INTELLIGENCE SUMMARY
APRIL 1919

(Erase heading not required.)

Instructions regarding War Diaries and Intelligence Summaries are contained in F.S. Regs., Part II. and the Staff Manual respectively. Title pages will be prepared in manuscript.

Place	Date	Hour	Summary of Events and Information	Remarks and references to Appendices
HARFLEUR	9th		General Routine	R.1
	10th		General Routine	R.2
	11th		General Routine. 1 Sergt. 3 men sent for dispersal.	R.1
	12th		General Routine. 1 men sent for dispersal.	R.2
	13th		Coys attached Divns Dismd – Lemon forwarded by the Regt Rwd. to Bishop of KHARTOUM. Lieut A.E. MAYLEY and Lieut P.C. TULLEY "E Buffs" attached and 1 man sent for dispersal.	R.1
	14th		General Routine – Instructions received 18th Middlesex Regt arriving probably on 15th inst are to take over No. 1 Dispatch Camp thus releasing Army "C" Coys also a detachment at CINDER CITY releasing "B" and "D" Coys. Volunteers and Returnd men of this Battalion to proceed to ROUEN probably on 17th instant.	R.1

WAR DIARY

Army Form C. 2118.

Page 3

of 1st Bn "The Queens"

INTELLIGENCE SUMMARY. APRIL 1919

Place	Date	Hour	Summary of Events and Information	Remarks and references to Appendices
HARFLEUR	15		General Routine. Lieut (a/Capt) J.E. CORRY M.C. Lieut (a/Capt) K.M. EAST Lieut J.E. SHIPTON, Lieut E.A. FIELD 2 Sgts 2 Cpl 11 O.R. sent for dispersal.	R.N.
"	16		General Routine.	R.N.
"	17		General Routine - 2 Sergts 2 Cpls. 9 men sent for dispersal	R.N.
"	18		General Routine - Relief of Companies by 18th Middlesex Regt. being carried out.	R.N.
"	19			R.N.
"	20		Battalion attended Divine Service. 1 man sent for dispersal.	R.N.
"	21		Have received that all returnable officers and other ranks for posting to 6th Battn will entrain at GARE MARITIME at 10.00 hours 22nd Instant.	R.N.
"	22		The Battalion (less Cadre) strength 20 officers 731 other ranks posted to 6th	R.N.

Army Form C. 2118.

WAR DIARY
APRIL 1919

INTELLIGENCE SUMMARY. of Bath. "THE QUEEN'S" Regt.

Page 4

Place	Date	Hour	Summary of Events and Information	Remarks and references to Appendices
HARFLEUR	22		Battalion. Companies marched independently – "A" and "C" from No. 1. Augustin Camp SANVIC, "B" from BELGIAN COMPOUND, SOUVENEVE. "D" from CINDER CITY and assembled at GARE MARITIME at 10.00 hours under Captain F.A.G. POWELL JONES M.C. Train was in waiting and Troops entrained at once when settled in their carriages, the Band which was in readiness on the platform struck up and played popular tunes until the train steamed out – as the Train moved slowly by the Regtl March "BRAGANZA" and "AULD LANG SYNE" were played by the Band. Prior to leaving their Duntero a message from Brigadier General L.J. WYATT, D.S.O. Commanding 98th Infy Bde. in which he regretted owing to observance from the station he was unable to address them personally, but on their being to join the 6th Battn with the 192nd Brigade he wished to express his appreciation of the splendid behavior – general smartness and turn out of also the good work done by the Battalion whilst attached to his Brigade since January 4th, was read to all ranks.	

WAR DIARY

APRIL 1919

INTELLIGENCE SUMMARY. 1st Batn. "THE QUEEN'S"

Army Form C. 2118.
Page 5.

(Erase heading not required.)

Place	Date	Hour	Summary of Events and Information	Remarks and references to Appendices
HARFLEUR	22		Ranks posted to 6th Battn. on this date were returned as follows:—	
			"ENTRAINED"	
			Captains F.A.G. POWELL-JONES M.C. P.A.WATTS. Lieut. T.CUMMINS. Lieut. C.E. LOVE. 2/Lieut. W. NORTHWOOD (R.SUSSEX att.)	
			A.J. SHEARLOCK. R.F.K. ROBERTS. J.H. TINDALL. W. STRINGER. T. WARD D.C.M. F. RAWLINSON. E. Surrey Regt att.	
			Total Officers 11. Other ranks 421.	
			"ON LEAVE"	
			Lieut J. RUDKIN, M.C.	
			Lieut W.E. LAWRENCE, M.C. P.E. TENNYSON, M.C. M.F. EPPS. H.C. ALLEN. B.B. ANTHONY. Total Officers 6. O.R. 243. The Buffs att. (R.W. Kents Regt att.) The Buffs att.	
			HOSPITAL— Other ranks 10. { On Command. 2/Lieuts. C.H.J. BENTLEY. H.C. CRAWLEY. A.C. BATTSON { Total Officers 3. Other ranks 35.	
			Two men sent for dispersal. Officers and other ranks of Calne and those awaiting dispersal assembled at Camp 23, 1st Battn. W.R. Kr.	
—"—	23		General Routine — One man sent for dispersal.	Kr.
—"—	24		General Routine — Captain R.M. MADDOCK M.C. sent for dispersal — Lieut. HELDYNE Discharged totally on leave R. Fraud Pb. Marlboro.	Kr.

WAR DIARY

APRIL 1919

INTELLIGENCE SUMMARY of Bath. "THE QUEEN'S"

(Erase heading not required.)

Army Form C. 2118.

Page 6.

Place	Date	Hour	Summary of Events and Information	Remarks and references to Appendices
HARFLEUR	25		General Routine — All Animals on Battalions charge handed in to R No 2 Remount Dept. — Two men sent for dispersal.	Apx
— " —	26		General Routine. —	Apx
— " —	27		Attended Divine Service. One man sent for dispersal.	Apx
— " —	28		General Routine	Apx
— " —	29		General Routine	Apx
— " —	30		General Routine. Particulars of re-enlistments carried out under A.O.IV of 9.12.18 and subsequent orders:— 2 " The Queen's Regt." on A.F.B. 2514—2. 1 Sgt. + Cpl. 4.3. 15. on A.F.B.2514—3. 3 Sgts. 2 Cpls. 11 Pte. On A.F.B. 2514—4. 1 Sgt. 2 Cpl. 5 Pte = Total 72. 1st "The East Kent Regt (The Buffs). on A.F.B.2514—2 = 5 Pte. on A.F.B.2514—3 = 4 Pte Total 9.	Apx

Army Form C. 2118.

Page 7.

WAR DIARY

INTELLIGENCE SUMMARY 1st Batt "THE QUEEN'S"

APRIL 1919

(Erase heading not required.)

Place	Date	Hour	Summary of Events and Information	Remarks and references to Appendices
			To the Norfolk Regt. — on A.F. B2514 – 3 = 2 R/o Total 2.	
			To the East Surrey Regt. — " — B 2514 – 2 = 1 " " 1.	
			To the Royal Sussex Regt. — " — B 2514 – 2 = 1 " " 1.	
			To the Hampshire Regt. — " — B 2514 – 2 . 1 P/o " m B 2514 – 3 = 2 P/o Total 5.	
			To the Devonshire Regt. — " — B 2514 – 3 = 1 " Total 1.	
			To the Essex Regt. — " — B 2514 – 3 = 1 " Total 1.	
			To the Northamptonshire Regt. — " — B 2514 – 2 = 4 " a B 2514 – 3 = 1 P/o Total 5.	
			To the King's Own (Y.L.I.) — " — B 2514 – 2 = 1 " Total 1.	
			To the Lincolnshire Regt. — " — B 2514 – 2 = 1 " Total 1.	
			To the Royal Munster Fus. — " — B 2514 – 4 = 2 " Total 2.	
			Grand Total 101.	M.

3rd April 1919.

H.B. Amery, Major
Comdg. 1st Bn "The Queen's" Regt N.S.

Army Form C. 2118.

WAR DIARY
of
INTELLIGENCE SUMMARY
(Erase heading not required.)

1st Battn "THE QUEENS" REGT.   Page 1.

MAY 1919   WR 55   40 T/Pws.

Instructions regarding War Diaries and Intelligence Summaries are contained in F. S. Regs., Part II. and the Staff Manual respectively. Title pages will be prepared in manuscript.

Place	Date	Hour	Summary of Events and Information	Remarks and references to Appendices
HARFLEUR	1st		General Routine — Troops confined to Camp Area except on duty. RM.	
—	2nd		General Routine. RM	
—	3rd		General Routine. 1 CQMS / Sgt sent for dispersal Cen	
—	4th		Strike attitude Divine Service. 2 C.d. M^s sent for dispersal. RM.	
—	5th		General Routine.	
—	6th		General Routine — 10 mins sent for dispersal RM.	
—	7th		General Routine — Instructions received re length of leave to be issued from 4 officers and 46 O.R. to 3 officers and 36 O.R. per authority H.Q. British Army on Rhine numbers oR./3192/Mot Gp 29 to 19. RM.	

(A6475) W. W2355/P367. 60,000 12/17 D. D. & L. Sch 532. Forms/C2118/13

Army Form C. 2118.
Page 2

WAR DIARY
INTELLIGENCE SUMMARY
of Batn. "THE QUEEN'S" Regt.

MAY 1919

Place	Date	Hour	Summary of Events and Information	Remarks and references to Appendices
HARFLEUR	8th		General Routine – 10 men sent to depôt for disposal – 3 Rank reenlisted for "The Queen's" Regt. for period 2 years and 3 months. Rn.	
"	9th		General Routine. Extracts from a provisional Order of Battle received under A.G. N°586/5 (MOB) dated April 1919 shows the Battalion under "5th Division" Rn.	
"	10th		General Routine. Rn.	
"	11th		Divine Service – 3 men sent for disposal Rn.	
"	12th		General Routine. Rn.	
"	13th		General Routine. Rn.	
"	14th		General Routine. Orders received Cadre to be prepared to embark immediately. Reminder to be sent to 6th Batn. Pr. Trinity. Rn.	
"	15th		Instructions received Cadre to embark on S.S. LYDIA this day. Vehicles loaded and placed on board the S.S. WARYARE by 12.00 hrs. 24 N.C.O. & men joined from 6th Battalion and taken on strength of Cadre replacing a similar	

Army Form C. 2118.

Page 5

WAR DIARY
or
INTELLIGENCE SUMMARY. 1st Batn. The Queen's Regt.

MAY 1919

(Erase heading not required.)

Instructions regarding War Diaries and Intelligence Summaries are contained in F. S. Regs., Part II. and the Staff Manual respectively. Title pages will be prepared in manuscript.

Place	Date	Hour	Summary of Events and Information	Remarks and references to Appendices
HARFLEUR	15th Continued		Number or Officers & rank & file – who were posted to 6th Battalion. At about 16.15 hours instructions were received for Cars and Bands to march to the QUAI d'ESCALE where embarkation would be carried out at once on arrival. The party paraded at 17.00 hours arrived at the Boat side at 19.00 hours and embarked immediately – A nominal Roll of same is appended. The Brigade Commander – Brig. Gen. L.J. WYATT D.S.O. accompanied by Captain C.W. BEART M.C. Staff Captain attended during embarkation of the Queens (1st Bn Middlesex Regt. and Seaforth, Argyll and Sutherland Highlanders were also on board) and bade farewell and God-speed to all ranks.	

H B Avery
Major

Comdg 1st Bn the Queens Regt

22.5.19

www.ingramcontent.com/pod-product-compliance
Lightning Source LLC
Chambersburg PA
CBHW081237170426
43191CB00034B/1701